Simon & Schuster
Modular Science
Key Stage 4

Electricity and Magnetism

Jim Breithaupt

Acknowledgements

The author and publishers would like to thank the following for permission to use photographs:

Britannia Fire Ltd 1.15; CEGB cover, 8.9, 8.12a and b; Mary Evans Picture Library 3.8; Sally & Richard Greenhill 7.16; IGE Medical Systems Ltd 9.1a; Intercity 5.2; Ander McIntyre 3.14, 4.8, 5.10, 7.19, 8.12c; NASA 9.1b; Steve Newman 7.8; Peugeot-Talbot 1.1b; John Radcliffe Hospital, Oxford 9.7; Rockwool 8.25; Ann Ronan Picture Library 1.13, 2.6, 6.6, 8.1; RS Components Ltd 2.7a, 6.9a, b and c, 7.13; Science Photo Library 1.11 (David Guyon/BOC), 9.2, 9.3 (Stammers/Thompson), 9.6 (Chris Priest); Louise Stewart 5.1, 5.9, 5.16; Topham Picture Source 1.1; Graham Topping 5.8; Unilab 7.12; John Walmsley 1.2; Wind Energy Group Ltd title page, 8.24.

First published in 1992 in Great Britain by
Simon & Schuster Education
Campus 400, Maylands Avenue
Hemel Hempstead, Herts HP2 7EZ

British Library Cataloguing in Publication Data
Breithaupt, Jim
Electricity and magnetism.
1. Electricity and magnetism
I. Title
537
ISBN 0 7501 0178 4

Designed and illustrated by
Ian Foulis & Associates
Saltash
Cornwall
Printed in Hong Kong by Wing King Tong Co. Ltd

Contents

Preface

To the teacher:
This book, as part of **Blackwell Modular Science for Key Stage 4**, covers all aspects of electricity and magnetism (AT11) in the National Curriculum from levels 7 to 10. It builds on the **Blackwell Modular Science for Key Stage 3** titles *Electricity, Magnetism and Micro-electronics 1 and 2* to prepare students for GCSE (or equivalent) examinations in science.

Activities including practical explorations and IT exercises are a major feature of the book and difficult concepts are developed and explained through practical exercises. Important discoveries are linked to the lives and work of the scientists who made them thus helping to develop further understanding of the subject as well as giving a wider appreciation of scientific methods.

To the student:
Electricity is used by each and every one of us in our daily lives. Without it, lots of activities would not be possible. Because electricity is so important, we need to know how to use it safely and efficiently. We are all consumers of electricity. This book will help you make good use of electricity.

Many jobs and careers involve working with electricity. Craftspeople, technicians, scientists and engineers working in industry, hospitals, laboratories and many other places all use knowledge and skills involving electricity.

- Who will keep our electricity supplies in operation in the future?
- Who will design, make, sell and service electrical appliances?

The short answer is *you*! As you work through this book, remember that people with skills and knowledge about electricity are needed to enable us all to keep using electricity. Find out more about careers involving electricity from your careers teacher.

Unit 1

Static electricity

30 December 1975

The Berge Istra

Yesterday a ship called the *Berge Istra* disappeared without trace. The ship was carrying almost 200 000 tonnes of iron ore from Brazil to Tokyo when it sank in calm seas near the Philippines. All except two members of the 32-strong crew lost their lives. The survivors reported three massive explosions within the space of 30 seconds. The ship took less than three minutes to sink. The *Berge Istra*, built in 1972, was an ore and oil carrier. On the previous voyage the ship had taken oil to Europe, where the tanks were cleaned and filled with inert gas.

Figure 1.1 Twenty-three crew were feared dead after this explosion off Tokyo Bay, 1989

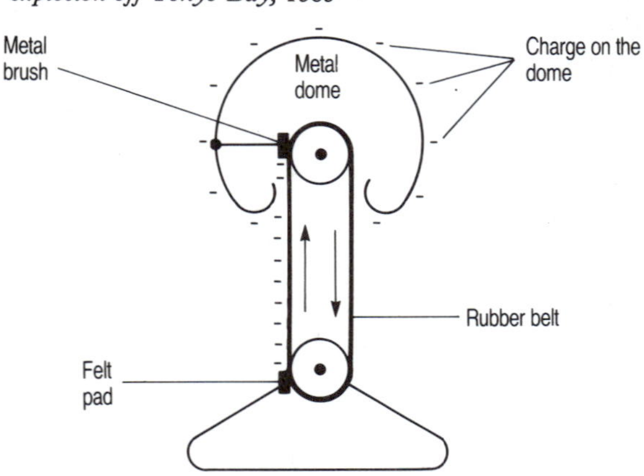

Figure 1.3 The Van der Graaff generator

1.1 Shocks and sparks

- What could have caused the explosions?

Some explosive vapour from the oil may have remained after the tanks were cleaned. Just a tiny spark could have caused this to ignite (see Figure 1.1).

Figure 1.2 Generating sparks

Making sparks

To prevent sparks, we need to know how they can be produced. The **Van der Graaff generator** (in Figure 1.2) is capable of generating massive sparks from its dome. Figure 1.3 shows how it works. The belt brushes continuously against a felt pad near the base of the generator. Friction between the pad and the belt causes the belt to become charged. The charge is carried up to the dome and spreads evenly across the dome's outer surface.

If a metal object is moved near the dome, a spark jumps from the dome to the object. The spark is a **discharge** of electricity from the dome.

Inside the atom

Every uncharged atom consists of three types of particle – **protons, neutrons** and **electrons**. The protons and neutrons make up the nucleus of the atom. The electrons are held in the atom by the force of attraction

		Charge	Mass
Proton	⊕	+	1
Neutron	○	0	1
Electron	○	-	$\frac{1}{1850}$

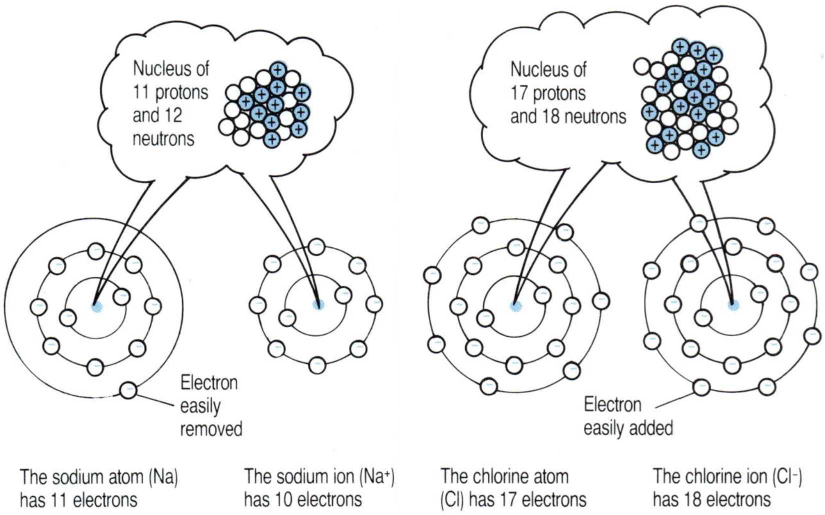

a *Sodium* **b** *Chlorine*

Figure 1.6 Atoms and ions

from the nucleus. Figure 1.6 shows the atomic compositions of sodium and chlorine.

Atoms become charged by removing or adding electrons. A charged atom is called an **ion**. For example a sodium atom easily loses an electron to become a positive ion. A chlorine atom easily gains an electron to become a negative ion.

Insulators such as polythene and Perspex become charged by friction. Rubbing a Perspex rod removes electrons from its surface atoms, so it becomes positively charged. Rubbing a polythene rod adds electrons to its surface atoms, so it becomes negatively charged.

Conductors contain atoms from which some electrons have escaped. These electrons move about freely inside the conductor. When an electric current passes through a conductor, these electrons move towards the positive end. They are replaced by electrons entering the conductor from the negative end.

Pipe problems

When oil or petrol is pumped from a road tanker into a storage tank, charge is created in the connecting pipe. If this charge builds up on the pipe, it could make sparks which could ignite the vapour and cause an explosion.

Static electricity can also be produced as a result of pumping grains of powder through pipes. The grains rub against each other and against the pipe wall, becoming charged due to friction. This effect is shown in Figure 1.7 (overleaf). Pouring powder down the pipe makes the electroscope leaf rise. This happens because the grains of powder become charged. The charged grains pile up in the can on the electroscope, making the electroscope charged.

Activity 1.1

Investigating charging by friction

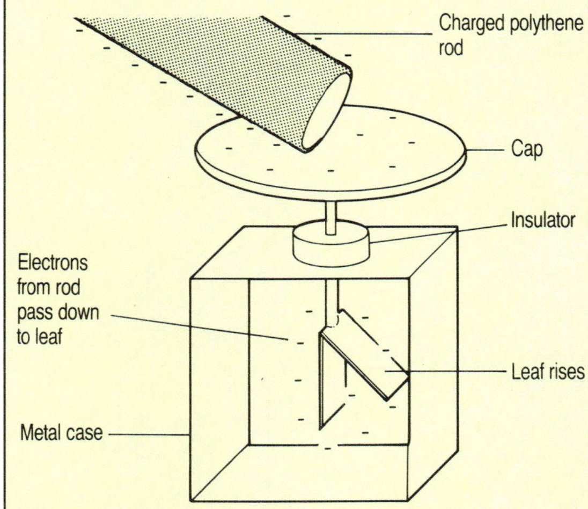

Figure 1.4 Charging an electroscope

Certain insulating materials become charged easily when rubbed with a dry cloth.

1. Rub a polythene rod on a dry cloth. Touch the rod on the cap of a **gold-leaf electroscope** and you will see that the electroscope leaf rises (see Figure 1.4). Charge from the rod spreads on to the electroscope. The leaf rises because it gains the same charge as the 'stem' of the electroscope and so is repelled by the stem. The rod becomes charged because it gains electrons from the cloth. Since electrons carry negative charge, the rod becomes negatively charged.
2. Now rub a Perspex (ie acetate) rod on a dry cloth and hold this rod over the charged electroscope. The leaf falls because the Perspex rod carries positive charge (see Figure 1.5). Holding the rod over a negatively charged electroscope attracts electrons up to the cap from the leaf. The Perspex rod loses electrons when rubbed with a dry cloth. This is why it becomes positively charged.

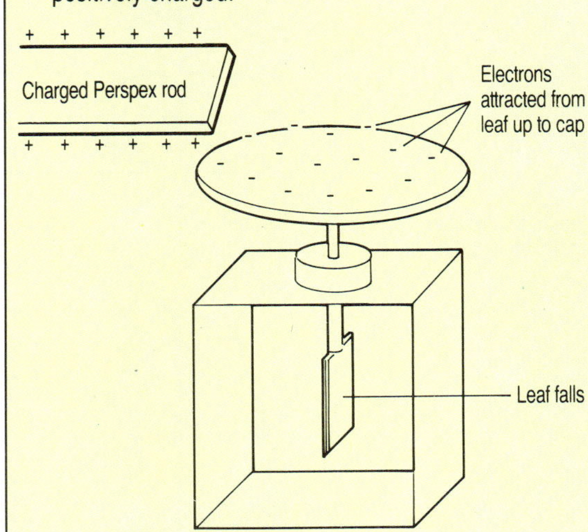

Figure 1.5 Making the leaf fall

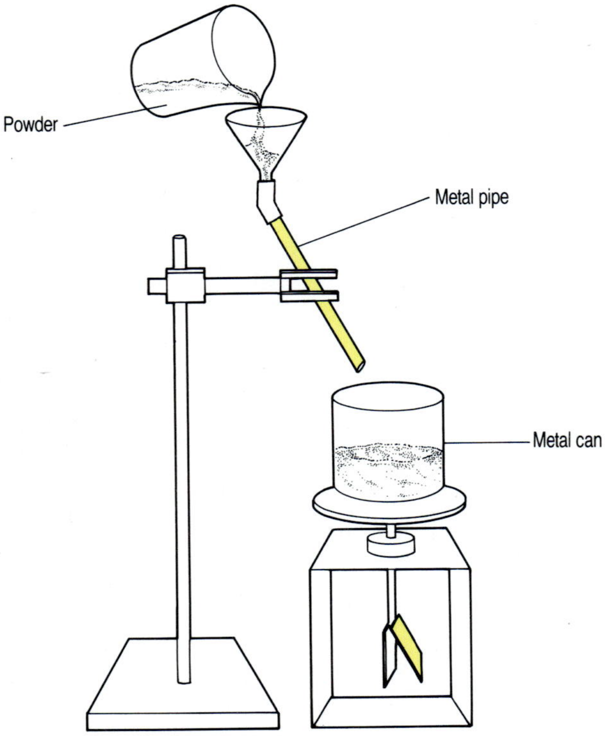

Figure 1.7 Charging powder grains

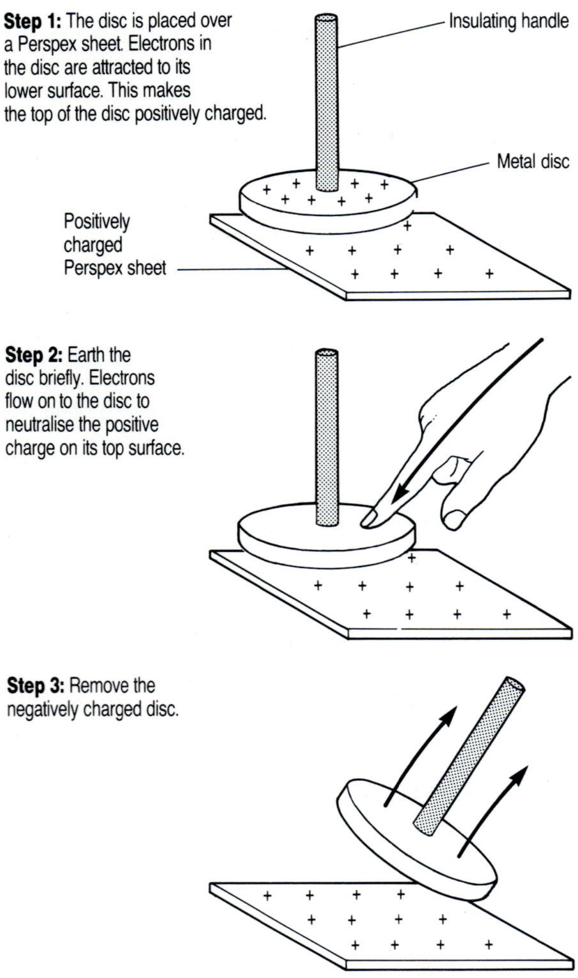

Figure 1.8 Charging by induction

Summary

Certain insulators can be charged by friction. An insulated metal can be charged positively or negatively by the transfer of electrons.

Questions

1 A polythene rod, rubbed with a dry cloth, becomes negatively charged.
  a Does the rod gain or lose electrons?
  b Does the cloth gain or lose electrons?
  c Why does the charge stay on the rod?

2 Explain each of the following tests:
  a A negatively charged rod is suspended horizontally from a thread. A second rod is brought near it. The rods repel each other.
  b The test is repeated after one hour but the rods no longer repel each other.
  c If the cap of a gold-leaf electroscope is touched with a charged rod, the leaf rises.

3 Copy and complete the following paragraph using the words at the end of the question:
  An uncharged atom has an equal number of __________ and electrons. The protons in an atom form part of the __________ of the atom. The electrons in an atom are held in place by the __________ force of the nucleus. Insulators that easily gain electrons become __________ charged whereas insulators that easily lose electrons become __________ charged.
  positively   negatively   nucleus   protons   attractive

4 In Figure 1.7, some fine-grain powdered milk is poured down the pipe.
  a Explain why this makes the electroscope leaf rise.
  b After the powder has been poured down the pipe, the leaf stays up. A positively charged rod brought near the electroscope cap then makes the leaf go up further. What type of charge did the powder gain?

1.2 Links and leaks

Charging up

A metal object can hold charge only if it is insulated from the Earth. One way of charging an insulated metal object is to touch it with a charged rod. Electrons are transferred between the rod and the metal object at the point of contact.

Another way of charging an insulated metal object is shown in Figure 1.8. This process is called **charging by induction**. There is no direct contact between the charged sheet and the metal disc. The metal disc is held over the charged sheet and briefly earthed. Electrons transfer between the disc and earth to charge the disc. After the earth link is removed, the charge remains on the disc. The sign of the charge on the disc is opposite to the sign of the charge on the sheet. Figure 1.9 shows how to charge an electroscope by induction.

Earthing

Touch a charged electroscope briefly and you will see that the leaf drops. This happens because the charge on the electroscope 'leaks' to the ground through you. (Perhaps you could use this to test whether you are a good conductor?)

Earthing a metal tank prevents charge building up on it. This is done by connecting a conducting link between the ground and the tank. A wire connecting the tank to a pipe which runs into the ground is a good link.

Suppose some powder is pumped into the tank, causing the tank to gain positive charge from the powder. Electrons from earth pass up the wire link to the tank to neutralise the positive charge. A different powder might give the tank negative charge. If this happens, electrons pass down the link to earth to keep the tank neutral.

Daily Gleaner

Bakery explodes!

Two people are in hospital today after an explosion at a local bakery. The accident happened as flour was pumped from a road tanker into a storage tank. Accident investigators think that a spark caused the powder in the tank to explode. They think the earth wire to the tank had become disconnected.

Antistatic floors

In a hospital operating theatre, patients are given anaesthetic gases during operations. These gases are usually supplied in steel cylinders and their use is carefully controlled by anaesthetists.

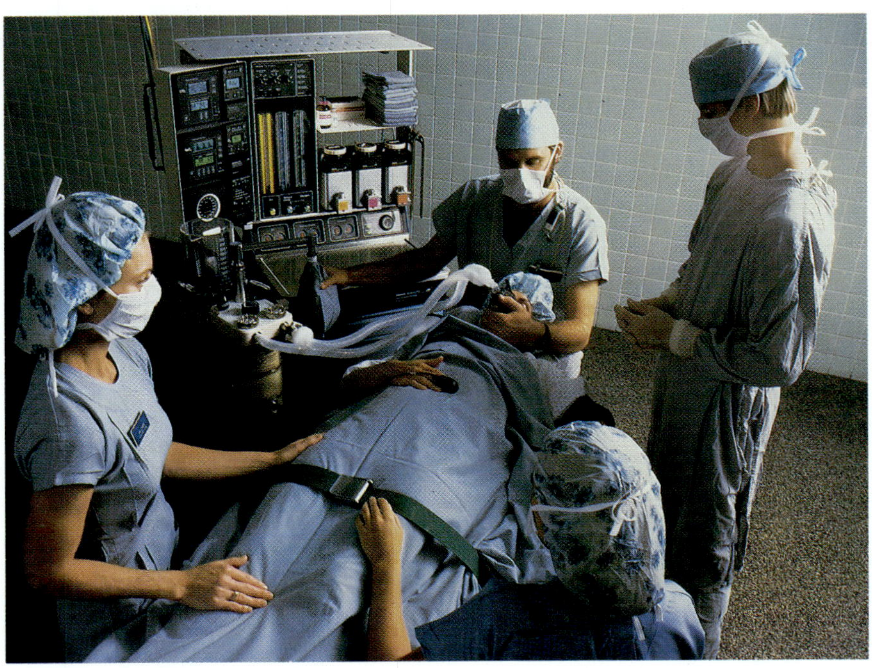

Figure 1.11 Inside an operating theatre

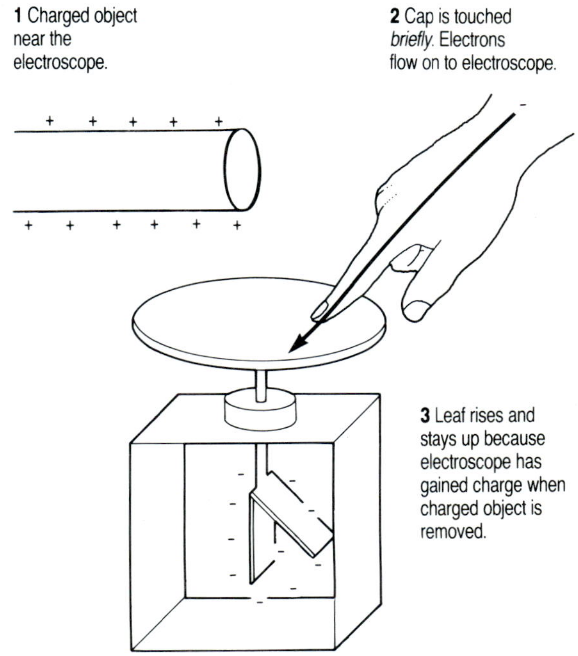

Figure 1.9 Charging an electroscope

Activity 1.2

Investigating earthing

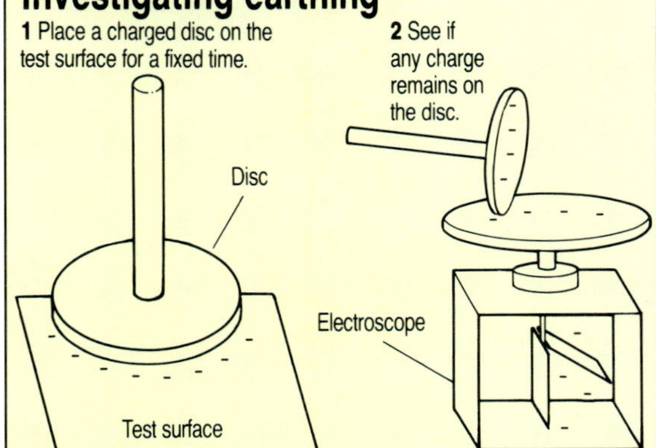

Figure 1.10 Testing different surfaces

A metal tank resting on a floor is not earthed if the floor is an insulator. Lots of floor coverings are insulators. Test different surfaces as follows to see which ones are good insulators.

1. Charge a metal disc by induction, as shown in Figure 1.8. Place the disc in contact with the test surface for 5 seconds (see Figure 1.10). Then use an electroscope to see whether it is still charged.
2. Repeat the test holding the disc on the test surface for different 'contact times'. Record your observations.
3. Try the test on some other surfaces including paper, polythene and wood.
4. What do your results tell you? Write a brief report on your findings.

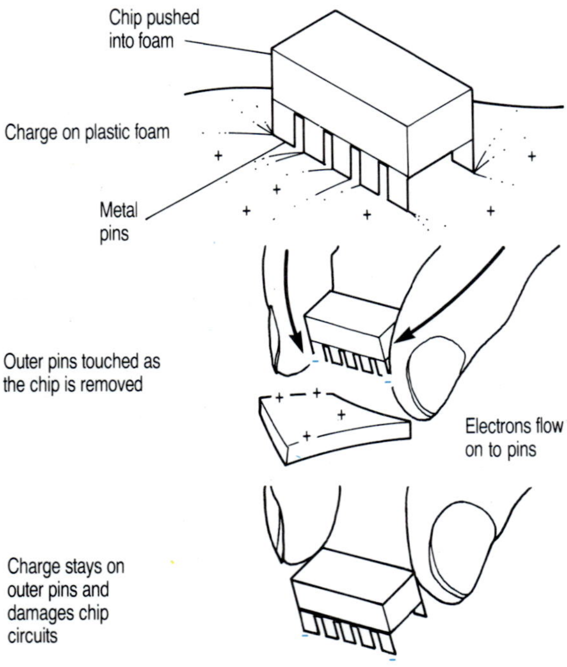

Figure 1.12 Chip damage by induction

Some anaesthetic gases such as ether are explosive. If the gas escapes and builds up in the air, an explosion could be triggered by a spark. To prevent charge building up on equipment in operating theatres, the floors have an antistatic surface. This conducts charge to earth. The material is essentially a poor insulator rather than a good conductor. A good conducting surface would put the theatre staff and patients at risk from electrocution. Why?

A chip problem

Computer chips can be damaged by static electricity. Most microcomputers contain **CMOS chips**. Tiny amounts of charge on the pins of a CMOS chip can destroy its electrical properties. To prevent chips being damaged by static electricity, manufacturers insert them into antistatic foam sheets before packaging them. This material is a conductor, so it stops the pins becoming charged.

Removing a chip by hand from ordinary plastic foam can charge the chip. Figure 1.12 shows how this happens if part of the foam is charged. If the pins are touched briefly with a finger while the chip is being removed, electrons pass on to the pins from earth, attracted by the oppositely-charged foam. Charge is **induced** on the pins. Antistatic foam does not retain charge, so protects the chip from damage.

Special tools are available to transfer chips to and from circuits. If these tools are used, the chips do not need to be handled. A chip could be charged by induction if it was handled near a charged surface.

Summary

Connecting a metal object to earth prevents it becoming charged. Antistatic materials are used to prevent damage to chips and to ensure safety in operating theatres.

Questions

1 Helen has just had a shock. She got up from a plastic chair to open the door and got an electric shock when she touched the door handle.
- **a** How did she become charged?
- **b** Why did she feel a shock when she touched the door handle?

2 A gold-leaf electroscope is charged by induction using a positively-charged rod.
- **a** What type of charge does the electroscope gain from this process?
- **b** Has the electroscope gained or lost electrons?
- **c** A negatively-charged rod is brought near the charged electroscope. Does the leaf rise or fall?

3
- **a** An insurance company has decided to safeguard its microcomputers by putting them on antistatic mats. What is the purpose of these mats?
- **b** The mats are then connected to a heating pipe which is earthed. Why?
- **c** How could you test a heating pipe to see if it is earthed?

4 **a** How would you show that cotton is a better antistatic material than nylon or Terylene?
b Threatre staff in hospitals wear gowns made of cotton. Why?
c Static electricity does not build up in a humid atmosphere. This is because an invisible film of water covers all objects in a humid atmosphere. Why does this prevent static electricity building up?

5 Write a letter to the *Daily Gleaner* about the bakery explosion outlining measures that might have prevented the earth wire becoming disconnected.

1.3 Using electric charges

The lightning conductor

Lightning never strikes in the same place twice – or does it? Benjamin Franklin (see Figure 1.13) was an American scientist who made important discoveries on the subject in the seventeenth century. He showed how lightning conductors discharge thunderclouds. His technique involved flying a kite below a thundercloud which is definitely not recommended!

In a thunderstorm, people caught in the open often run for shelter under a tree. This is not to be recommended either, since lightning is more likely to hit a tree than to hit open ground.

A lightning strike is a massive flow of charge between a thundercloud and the ground. Clouds become charged when hot air currents mix with cold air in the atmosphere. A lightning conductor on a tall building prevents lightning strikes by allowing the thunderclouds to discharge gradually.

Figure 1.13 Benjamin Franklin (1706–90) made many discoveries about static electricity. He was one of the first scientists to think of electricity in terms of tiny particles.

The action of points

The Van der Graaff generator is capable of producing massive sparks. If an earthed metal object is moved near the charged dome, a spark jumps from the dome to the object. The spark is like a lightning flash between a thundercloud and the ground.

A pin fixed to the dome would have prevented charge building up on it. Charge leaks off the tip of the pin. This happens because charge on the dome concentrates at the tip of the pin. Air molecules near the tip are pulled apart by the strong force between the charge on the pin and their electrons. The molecules are said to be **ionised** near the tip. Figure 1.14 shows how the ions created discharge the dome. This is called the **action of points**.

A lightning conductor discharges a thundercloud in the same way as the pin discharges the dome. The conductor is joined to the ground by a thick copper strip. This allows charge to pass between the conductor tip and the ground.

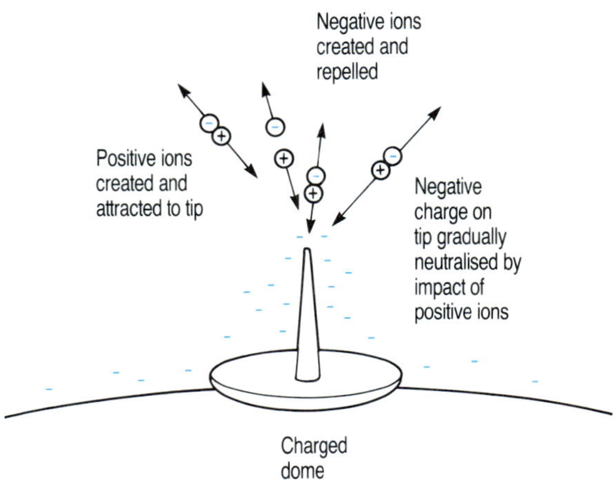

Figure 1.14 Action of points

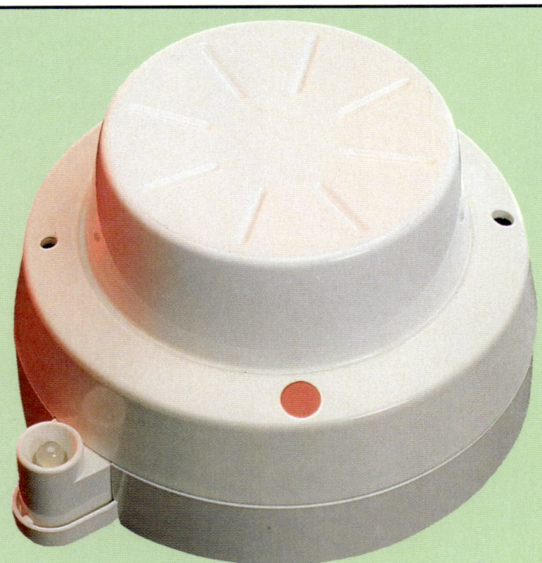

Figure 1.15 A smoke alarm

Applications:

The smoke alarm

Smoke alarms (see Figure 1.15) have a detector containing a very weak radioactive source that ionises the air in the detector. If smoke enters the detector, many more ions are produced and the alarm is triggered.

The automatic paint sprayer

Paint sprayers like that in Figure 1.16 are used to paint metal panels. The paint spray nozzle is connected to the positive terminal of an electrostatic generator. The negative terminal is connected to the metal panel which is earthed. Paint droplets from the spray are attracted on to the panel. This gives a uniform coating of paint on the panel.

Figure 1.16 An electrostatic paint sprayer

The electrostatic precipitator

Coal-fired power stations produce vast quantities of ash and dust. Electrostatic precipitators (see Figure 1.17) are used to remove them from the flue gases so they are not released into the atmosphere.

The particles of ash and dust pass through a grid of wires in the precipitator. The grid is at a high voltage so it charges the particles. They are then attracted on to charged metal plates instead of passing through the precipitator with the waste gases.

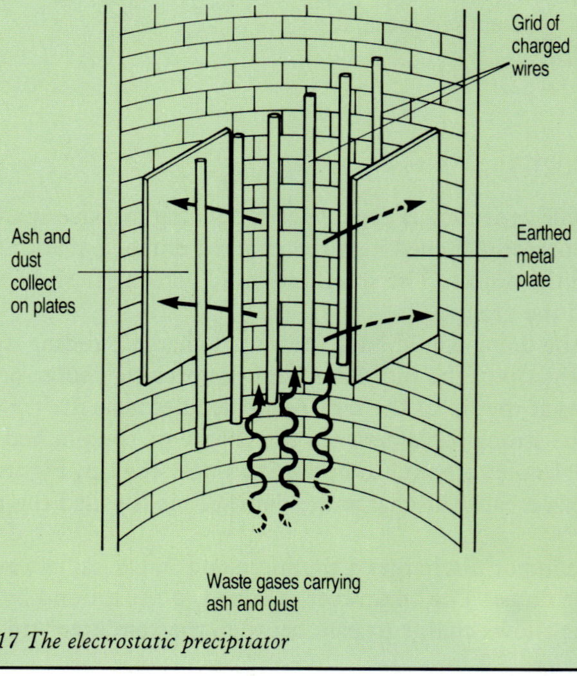

Figure 1.17 The electrostatic precipitator

The photocopier

To use a copier, all you need to do is to put the sheet to be copied in the machine and press a button. Within seconds, out comes a perfect copy. Although a copier is simple to use, the process involved in making a photocopy is quite involved, as Figure 1.18 shows.

Figure 1.18 How a photocopier works

Summary

The devices described above make use of the basic principles of static electricity.

Questions

1 a Why should smoke alarms always be fitted near ceilings rather than near floors?

b Why do you think smoke causes more ions to be produced in the detector?

2 a The automatic paint sprayer is not suitable for painting panels with sharp points. Why?

b Why must the panels being sprayed be earthed?

3 What are the benefits of removing ash and dust from a power station's flue gases?

4 Susan is using a photocopier and notices that the copies are becoming lighter and lighter. The powder cassette needs to be refilled.

a Why do the copies become lighter when there is insufficient powder in the cassette?

b She notices that the copies are sometimes charged. Why do you think this happens?

Unit 2

Charge and current

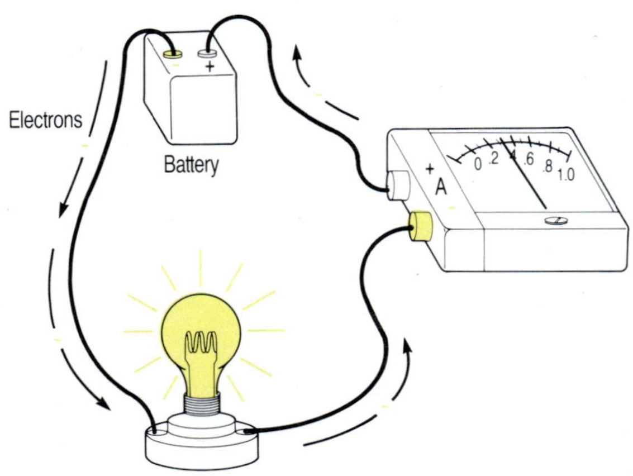

Figure 2.1 Using an ammeter

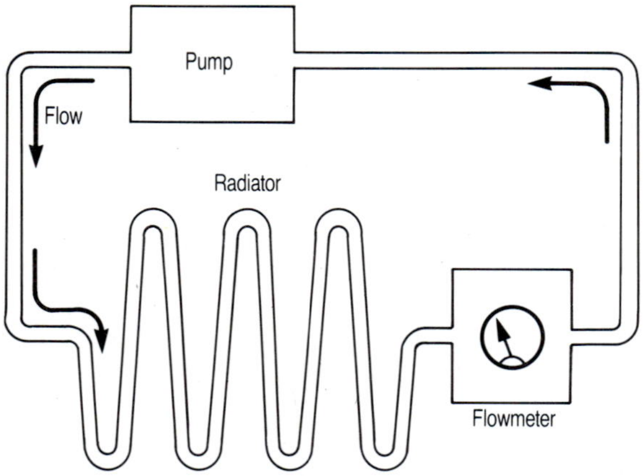

Figure 2.2 A water circuit

2.1 Electrons on the move

When a torch bulb is connected to a battery, the battery pushes electrons through it. Each electron has a tiny amount of negative charge. The flow of charge through the torch bulb is an **electric current**. It can be measured using an **ammeter** (see Figure 2.1). The **voltage** of the battery is a measure of the 'push' on each electron. The scale of an ammeter is marked in **amperes** (A). (The ampere is defined on page 58.) What is the reading on the ammeter in Figure 2.1?

An electric circuit is a bit like a water circuit. Figure 2.2 shows a flowmeter being used to measure the rate of water flow through the 'circuit'. The flowmeter in the water circuit is a bit like the ammeter in the electric circuit.

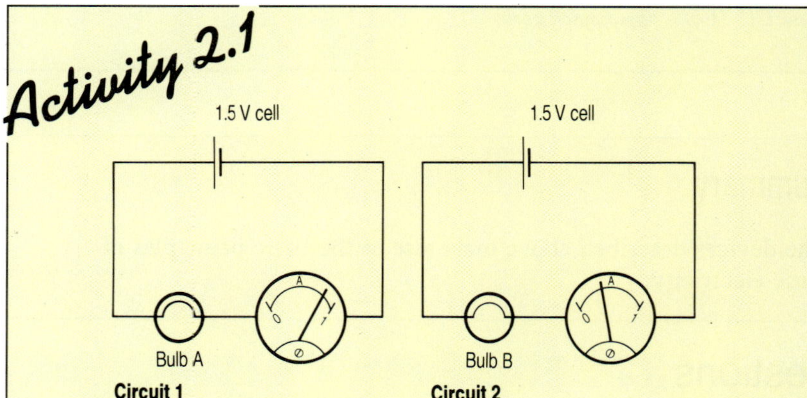

Figure 2.3 Comparing charge flow

Measuring charge

Figure 2.3 shows two torch-bulb circuits. Compare the ammeter readings. The current is the charge passing through the torch bulb each second.

- Which torch bulb passes most charge each second?

The charge passing through a torch bulb is given by the equation:

$$\text{Charge} = \text{current} \times \text{time}$$

Charge is measured in **coulombs** (or C for short). One coulomb is the charge passing through a torch bulb each second when the current is 1 A. So a charge flow rate of 1 coulomb per second is a current of 1 ampere.

Worked example

A current of 0.25 A passes through a bulb in a torch lamp when the lamp is switched on. How much charge passes through the bulb in 300 s?

Solution

Current = 0.25 A
Time = 300 s
Charge = current × time = 0.25 A × 300 s = 75 C

The charge of the electron

An ammeter reading 1 A passes charge at a rate of 1 coulomb per second. The charge is carried by electrons. Each electron carries a tiny amount of negative charge. More than six million million million electrons each second pass through an ammeter reading 1 A!

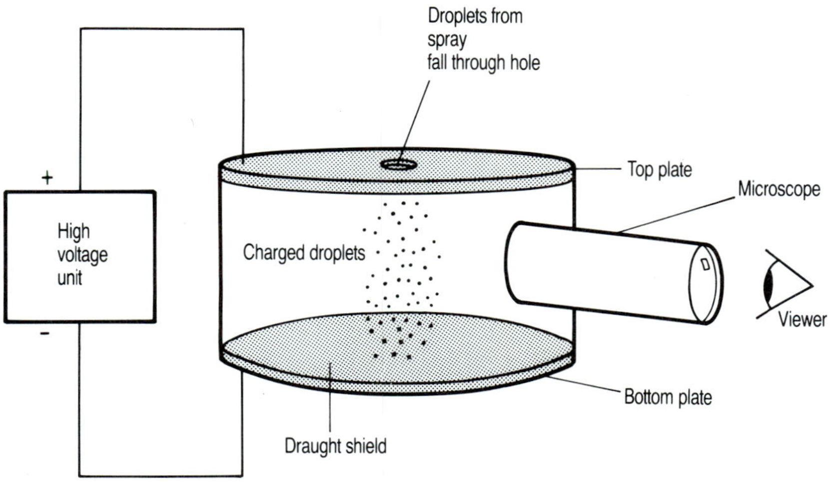

Figure 2.5 Measuring the charge of an electron

Robert Millikan, an American scientist, was the first person to measure the charge of the electron. He did this by observing single oil droplets sprayed between charged metal plates, as shown in Figure 2.5. The droplets become charged by the spraying process. Millikan measured the voltage needed to hold each droplet stationary. He then worked out the charge on each droplet. Here are some typical results from an experiment like this:

Droplet 1 3.2×10^{-19} C
Droplet 2 4.8×10^{-19} C
Droplet 3 1.6×10^{-19} C
Droplet 4 3.2×10^{-19} C

The charge on a droplet was always a whole number multiplied by 1.6×10^{-19} C. The smallest charge on a droplet was found to be 1.6×10^{-19} C. Millikan concluded that this is the charge of a single electron.

Summary

Charge is measured in coulombs. One coulomb is the charge passing each second along a wire carrying a current of 1 A. A single electron carries a charge of -1.6×10^{-19} C.

Activity 2.2

Investigating charge flow in circuits

1 Set up circuit 1 in Figure 2.4. Ask your teacher to check that you have wired the circuit correctly.

2 Close the switch and record the ammeter readings in a table like Table 2.1. Table 2.1 shows a set of sample measurements.

Circuit	Ammeter readings (A)		Battery current (A)
	A_1	A_2	
1	0.25	0.25	

Table 2.1

3 Repeat the measurements for the other circuits.

4 Work out the current passing through the battery in each case. Write your results in your table.

- For each circuit,

a how much charge passes through each ammeter in 100 s?

b how much charge leaves the battery in 100 s?

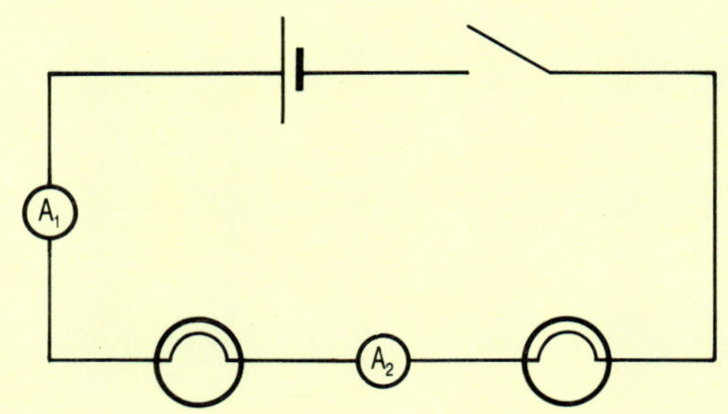

Circuit 1

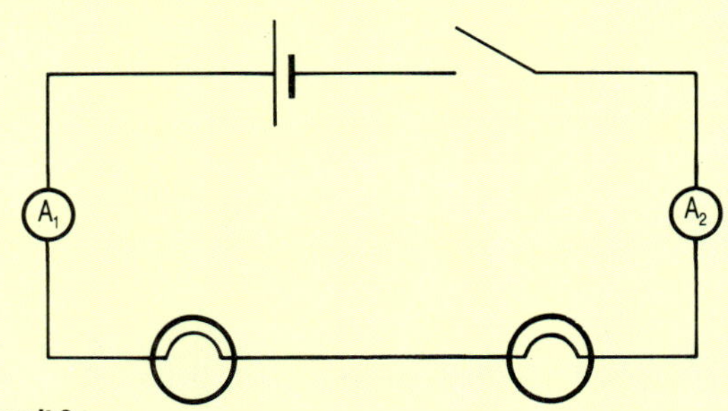

Circuit 2

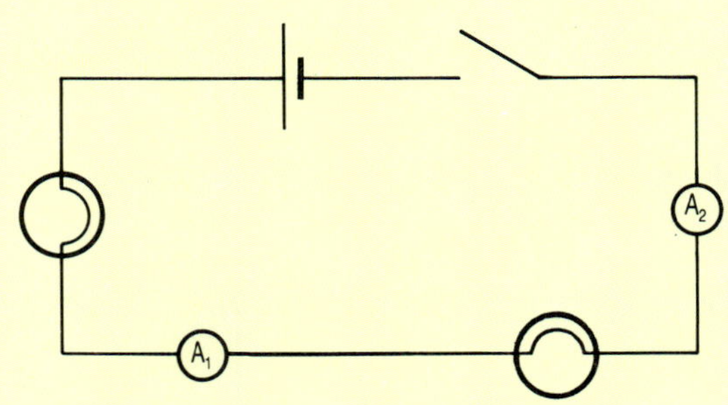

Circuit 3

Figure 2.4 Investigating circuits

Charles Coulomb (1736–1806)

Charles Coulomb (see Figure 2.6) was a French scientist who made important discoveries about magnetism, friction and electric charge. He showed how to measure charge. The unit of charge is named after him.

Figure 2.6 Charles Coulomb (1736–1806)

Questions

1 a A current of 0.35 A passes through a torch bulb. How much charge passes through it in **i** 1 s **ii** 100 s?

b The total charge passed through an ammeter was 75 C.
i What was the ammeter reading if the time taken was 25 s?
ii If the ammeter reading had been 2 A, how long would it have taken for 75 C to pass through it?

2 Daljit is unsure which of two cells to buy for his torch lamp. 'Lightit' gives a maximum current of 0.25 A for 10 hours. 'Brightist' gives 0.4 A for 6 hours.
a Which cell gives most charge?
b How much more charge is given by this cell?

3 a A current of 0.08 A passed through a human body is sufficient to cause electrocution. Work out the charge flowing when this current is passed for 0.001 s.
b How many electrons are needed to carry this amount of charge?

4 a How many electrons are needed to make a total charge of one coulomb?
b How many electrons are carried by an oil droplet carrying a charge of
i 3.2×10^{-19} C **ii** 8×10^{-19} C **iii** 4.8×10^{-19} C?

2.2 Storing charge

Capacitors (see Figure 2.7) are used to store charge. A pair of parallel plates connected to a battery stores charge. The plates act as a simple capacitor. Electrons from the negative terminal of the battery go on to one plate, making it negative. Electrons leave the other plate and flow into the battery at its positive terminal. This plate becomes positive. The amount of charge on the plates depends on the voltage of the battery used to charge the capacitor.

Practical capacitors can be made using two sheets of metal foil instead of metal plates. The sheets are insulated from each other and rolled up, as shown in Figure 2.7**d**.

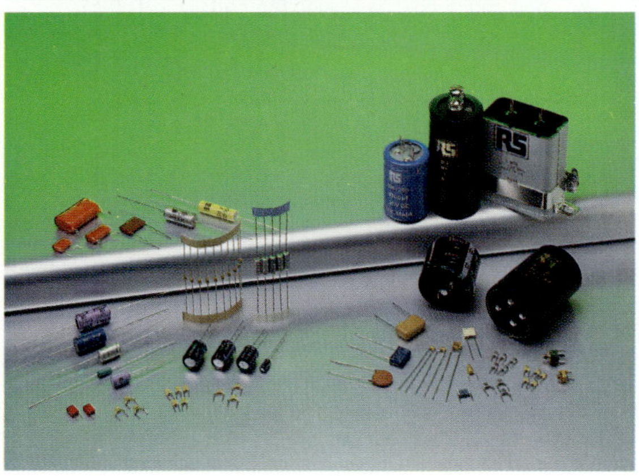

a *These are all capacitors*

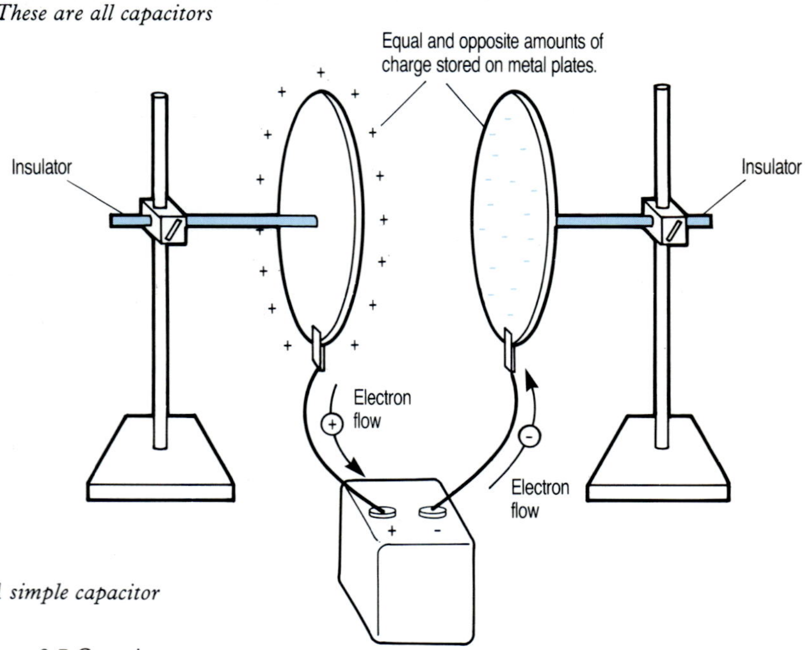

b *A simple capacitor*

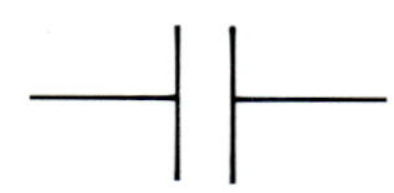

c *Capacitor symbol*

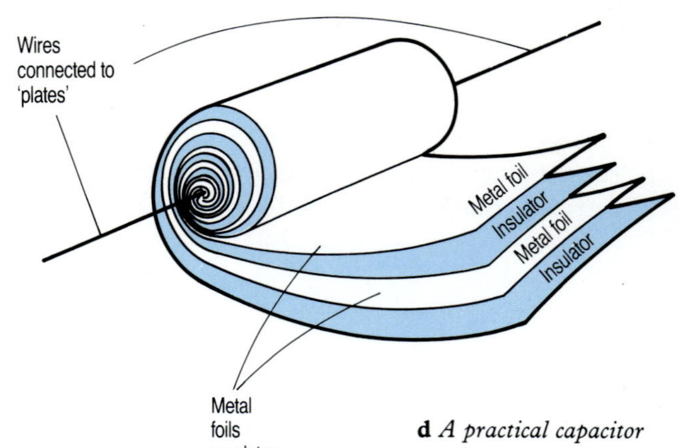

d *A practical capacitor*

Figure 2.7 Capacitors

Activity 2.3

Charging a capacitor

Set up the circuit of Figure 2.8 and try the following tests.

1 Close the switch and observe how the ammeter reading changes.

- What does this tell you about the flow of charge on to the capacitor?

2 Open and close the switch again.

- Why is the current zero when the switch is closed this time?

3 Open the switch and use a spare wire to short-circuit the capacitor terminals, as shown in Figure 2.8. Close the switch again and observe how the ammeter reading changes.

- Why is there a flow of charge this time?

4 Change the resistance of the variable resistor and repeat the tests.

- What difference does the change of resistance make?

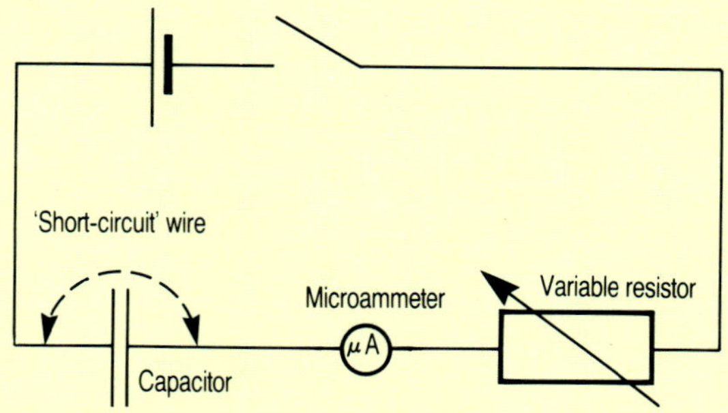

Figure 2.8 Charging a capacitor

Activity 2.4

Measuring charge stored

1 Use the circuit in Figure 2.8 to charge a capacitor at constant current. To do this, you will have to adjust the variable resistor continually to keep the ammeter reading constant.

2 With the aid of a friend, measure the current and the capacitor voltage at intervals after the switch is closed. Record your readings in a table. Some typical measurements are given in Table 2.2.

Current = 3×10^{-5} A

Time (s)	0	30	60	90	120
Voltage (V)	0	0.60	1.21	1.78	2.42

Table 2.2

In Table 2.2, the time taken to reach 0.6 V was 30 s. Since charge = current × time, the charge stored at 0.6 V was 3×10^{-5} A × 30 s = 9×10^{-4} C.

3 Work out from these results charge stored at 1.2 V. (You should find it is double the charge stored at 0.6 V.) Do your results show this?

Capacitance

The results of Activity 2.4 show that the charge stored is proportional to the voltage. In other words, the charge stored divided by the voltage is a constant. This is called the **capacitance** of the capacitor.

$$\text{Capacitance} = \frac{\text{charge stored}}{\text{voltage}}$$

Capacitance is measured in **farads** (F). One farad equals 1 coulomb per volt. Practical capacitors are usually labelled in **microfarads** ($1\ \mu F = 10^{-6}$ F).

Questions

1 A capacitor is connected in series with a **light-emitting diode** (LED), a switch and a battery.

a Sketch the circuit diagram.

b When the switch is closed, the LED lights up briefly. Explain why.

2 The circuit in Figure 2.8 can charge a capacitor at a constant rate.

a Why must the resistance of the variable resistor be reduced constantly to keep the current constant?

b What would happen if the resistance was not changed?

3 **a** Use the measurements in Table 2.2 to plot a graph of charge stored (on the vertical axis) against voltage.

b Read off from your graph the charge stored at **i** 1 V **ii** 2 V.

c Work out the capacitance of the capacitor in Figure 2.8.

4 How much charge is stored when a 1000 μF capacitor is charged to a voltage of **a** 1 V **b** 2 V **c** 10 V?

Summary

Capacitors are used to store charge. The capacitance of a capacitor is the charge stored per volt.

Unit 3

The chemical effects of electricity

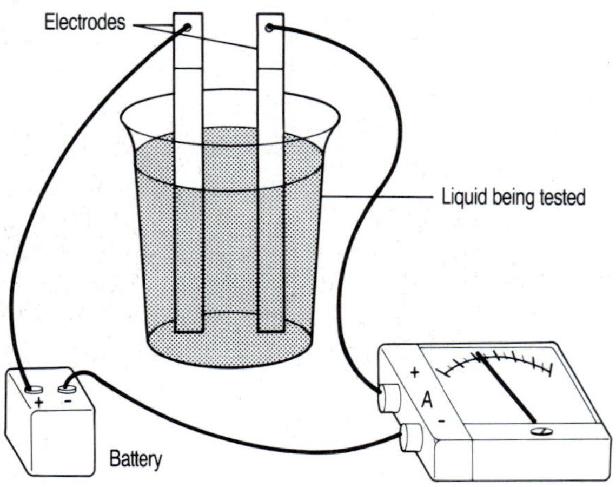

Figure 3.1 Conduction in liquids

3.1 Electrolysis

In winter in Britain, the demand for electricity is sometimes so high that electricity is 'imported' from France. It comes along electricity cables which have been laid between Britain and France across the bed of the English Channel. These cables have to be waterproofed because sea water conducts electricity.

Conduction by a liquid can be tested using the circuit shown in Figure 3.1. The terminals which pass electricity into the liquid are called **electrodes**. The ammeter reading shows whether the liquid conducts electricity.

Tests like this show that certain liquids such as oil, paraffin and pure (ie distilled) water do not conduct electricity. Other liquids, such as acids, salt solutions, tap water and sea water, do conduct electricity.

- Why do certain liquids conduct electricity while others do not?

One clue is to see what happens at the electrodes. You may see bubbles of gas at the electrodes, depending on which liquid is in the beaker.

When this happens, elements leave the liquid. The liquid is said to **decompose**. Decomposing a liquid by passing a current through it is called **electrolysis**. The beaker and the two electrodes make up an **electrolytic cell**. The liquid is called an **electrolyte**.

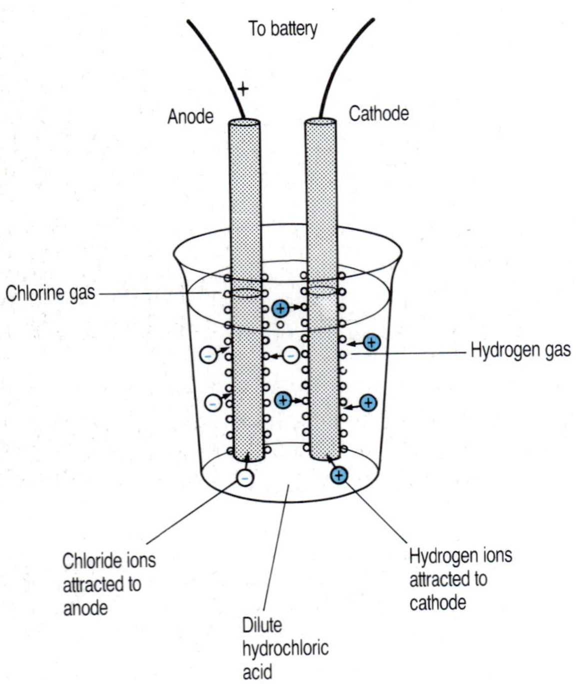

Figure 3.2 Electrolysis of dilute hydrochloric acid

Ions and atoms

An **ion** is a charged atom. Atoms can be charged by adding or taking away electrons. If electrons are added to an uncharged atom, the atom becomes a negative ion. To make a positive ion, electrons must be taken away from an uncharged atom.

Hydrogen and metal atoms easily lose electrons to form positive ions. Certain other atoms easily gain electrons to form negative ions. Ionic compounds such as metal salts and acids contain positive and negative ions. For example, sodium chloride contains sodium ions which are positive and chloride ions which are negative (see Figure 1.6, page 5). When the salt is dissolved in water, these ions can move about freely.

All acids contain hydrogen ions which are positive. The negative ions in an acid depend on the type of acid. For example, in hydrochloric acid the negative ions are chlorine atoms that have each gained a single electron.

- What happens when a battery is connected to the electrodes of an electrolytic cell (see Figure 3.2)?

1 The positive ions are attracted to the negative electrode. This electrode is called the **cathode**. Positive ions reaching the cathode take electrons from the cathode. They are 'discharged' and become neutral atoms.

2 The negative ions are attracted to the positive electrode. This electrode is called the **anode**. They give up electrons at the anode and become neutral atoms.

Activity 3.1

Investigating the conduction of tap water

Tap water conducts electricity because it contains dissolved solids. Plan and carry out an experiment to find out, by electrolysis, how much dissolved solid is in a certain volume of tap water. Here are some hints to help you.

1 Use the apparatus in Figure 3.1 to test the conduction of water containing known amounts of common salt in solution. You will need to make salt solutions of different known strengths. Work out the strength of each solution from the mass of salt dissolved divided by the volume of water used. Measure the current for each solution.

2 Plot your measurements on a graph.

3 Test tap water. Use the results and your graph to estimate the mass of solid dissolved in 1 cm^3 of tap water. Assume the dissolved solid conducts the same as common salt.

Metal plating

Metal ions are positive. In solution, in an electrolytic cell, they are always attracted to the cathode (ie the negative terminal). When metal ions are discharged at the cathode, they form a layer on the cathode.

Copper plating

Figure 3.3 shows a key being copper plated in a solution of copper(II) sulphate. A thin pink deposit is gradually formed on the key. This layer consists of copper from the copper(II) sulphate solution.

The longer the key is left in the circuit, the thicker the layer of copper on it. Increasing the current also makes the layer thicker. The layer becomes thicker as more and more atoms are attracted on to the cathode.

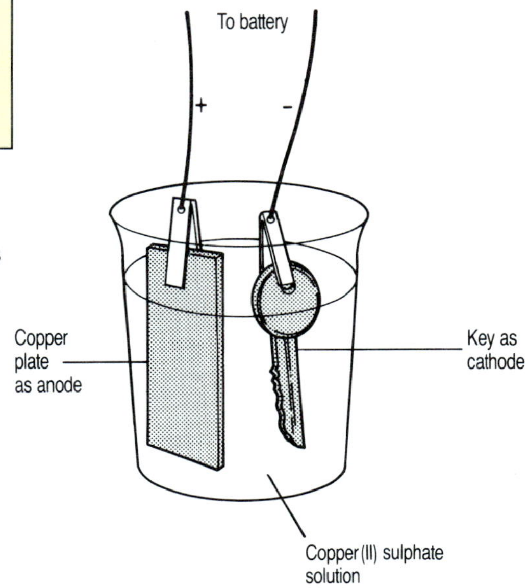

Figure 3.3 Copper plating

Applications:

Silver plating

Knives, forks and spoons are silver plated by electrolysis. The cultery acts as the cathode in an electrolytic cell which contains a solution of silver cyanide.

Silver ions are positive. In the electrolytic cell, they are attracted to the cathode where they form a layer of silver.

Chromium plating

A **micrometer** is a very accurate instrument capable of measuring thicknesses as small as 0.01 cm. If the surface layers of a micrometer wear away, it becomes inaccurate. To prevent this, the micrometer is coated with a protective layer of chromium. This is a metal much harder than steel. The coating is applied by making the micrometer the cathode of an electrolytic cell. Chromic acid is used as the electrolyte.

Summary

Electrolytic liquids contain positive and negative ions. Electrolysis causes liquids to decompose. In metal-plating processes, the object to be coated is used as the cathode in an electrolytic cell.

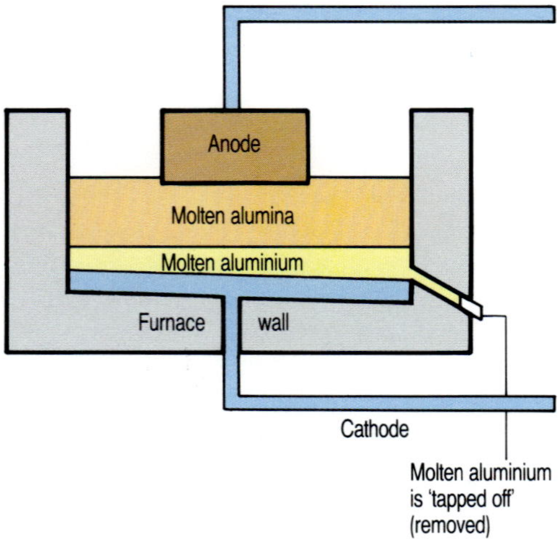

Figure 3.4

Questions

1 Jane wants to copper plate a key with her name. She intends to paint 'Jane' on the key and then copper plate the key. The paint does not react with copper(II) sulphate.
  a Will this work? Explain.
  b How will the key look after it has been copper plated?

2 **a** To copper plate a key, the key must be connected to the negative terminal of the battery. Why?
  b When current is passed through any acid, hydrogen gas is released at the cathode. What does this tell you about the type of charge carried by hydrogen ions?

3 Design a system to monitor the amount of dissolved solids in tap water as it flows through a copper pipe.

4 Make a list of objects that are metal plated. What type of metal is used in each case?

5 To make pure aluminium, a current is passed through molten aluminium oxide (alumina). Figure 3.4 shows the process. What would happen if
  a the voltage connections were the wrong way round
  b the furnace was switched off so it cooled down
  c the molten aluminium was not 'tapped off'?

3.2 Measuring electrolysis

If the coating on silver-plated cutlery is too thin, it is soon rubbed away by continual polishing. Manufacturers of metal-plated objects need to control the thickness of the coating carefully.

Activity 3.2

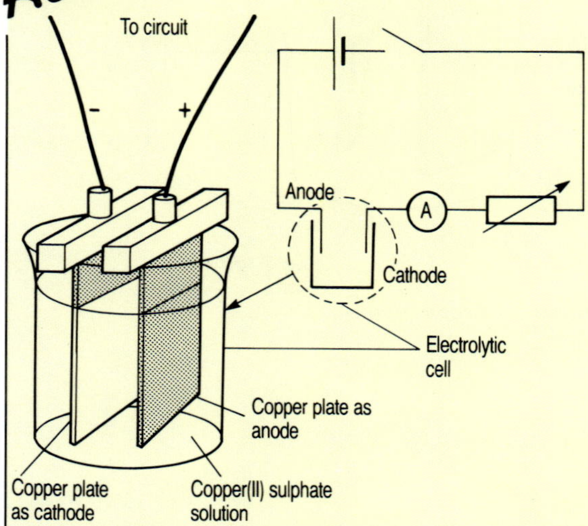

Figure 3.5 Investigating copper plating

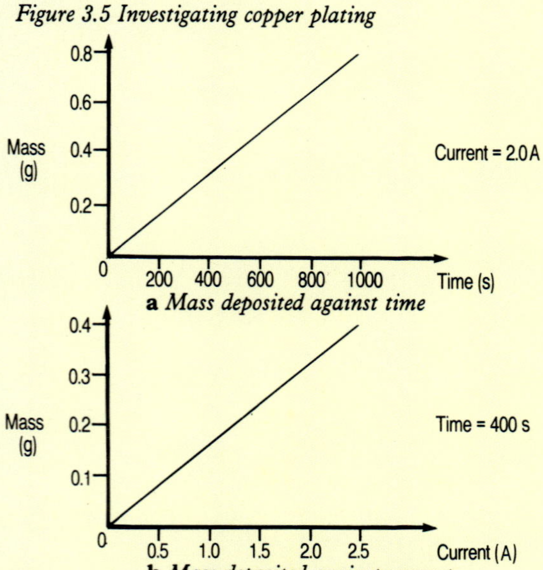

a *Mass deposited against time*

b *Mass deposited against current*

Figure 3.6 Typical results

Investigating copper plating

- What does the mass of copper which is deposited depend on? How does the mass depend on the current, the time taken and the strength of the copper(II) sulphate solution?

Figure 3.5 shows how you can investigate this.

1 Measure the mass of the copper plate to be used as the cathode. Then connect the plate into the circuit, close the switch and pass a measured current for a fixed time.
2 Remove the cathode and dry it without rubbing any copper off. Measure the mass of the cathode now and work out the gain in mass. Record your measurements.
3 Repeat the test using different currents for the same time. Different groups in a class could each try a different current.
4 If possible, try the same current for different times as well.
5 Plot the measurements as a graph of mass deposited (on the vertical axis) against current or time. Figure 3.6 shows some typical results.

The results in Figure 3.6 show that the mass deposited, m, is

- proportional to the current, I
- proportional to the time taken, t.

These links can be written as an equation

$$\text{Mass deposited} = \text{constant} \times \text{current} \times \text{time}$$

Since the charge passed is equal to current × time, then

$$\text{Mass deposited} = \text{constant} \times \text{charge passed}$$

6 Use your own measurements to work out the value of the constant in this equation.

Ions at work

● Why is the mass of copper deposited proportional to the charge passed? Each copper ion deposited on the cathode delivers a fixed amount of charge to the cathode. It also adds a fixed amount of mass to the cathode.

For N ions of copper deposited at the cathode,

Total charge delivered = $N \times$ charge of a single copper ion

Total mass deposited = $N \times$ mass of a single copper ion

The mass deposited is proportional to the number of ions. The total charge is also proportional to the number of ions. Therefore, the mass deposited is proportional to the charge passed.

Comparing the charges of different ions

Different elements can be produced by electrolysis. For example, oxygen is produced at the anode and hydrogen at the cathode when current is passed through acidified water. If hydrochloric acid is used as the electrolyte, hydrogen and chlorine gases are produced.

These investigations were first carried out over 150 years ago by Michael Faraday. He used the results to work out the charge carried by different ions. He discovered that 96 500 coulombs of charge are needed to release 1 g of hydrogen. Then he tested other elements to find out how much mass was released by this amount of charge. He compared the mass released with the atomic mass of the element.

For example, he discovered that the amount of charge needed to release 1 g of hydrogen is capable of releasing 35.5 g of chlorine or 31.5 g of copper. From atomic masses, he knew that 1 g of hydrogen contains the same number of atoms as 35.5 g of chlorine or 63 g of copper. From his electrolysis experiments, he knew that the same charge is carried by 1 g of hydrogen ions and 35.5 g of chloride ions (see Figure 3.7 and Table 3.1). Therefore the charge carried by a hydrogen ion is equal and opposite to that of a chloride ion. What do you think he discovered about the copper ion's charge compared with that of the hydrogen ion?

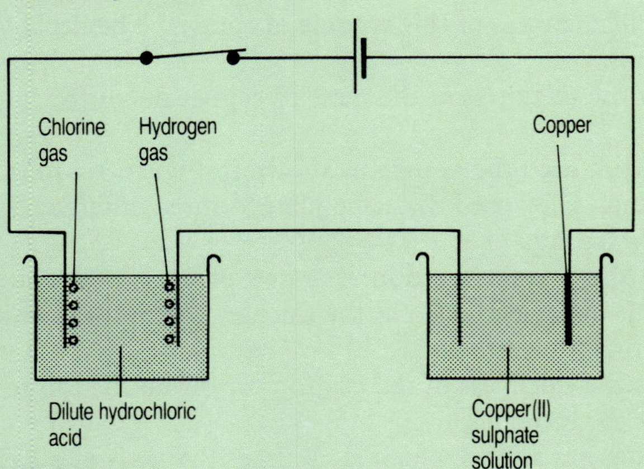

Figure 3.7 Comparing ions

	Chlorine	Hydrogen	Copper
Mass released	35.5 g	1.0 g	31.5 g
Atomic mass	35.5	1	63
Ion	Cl^-	H^+	?

Table 3.1

A scientific puzzle

Antoine Lavoisier was a famous French scientist who made many important discoveries, including the role of oxygen in combustion. He thought that oxygen was contained in all acids. This was investigated using electrolysis by Sir Humphry Davy (see Figure 3.8) in England. Davy could find no trace of oxygen in the gases produced when an electric current was passed through hydrochloric acid. This led him to conclude that Lavoisier's theory of acids was incorrect.

Figure 3.8 Sir Humphrey Davy lecturing at the Surrey Institution, 1809

Summary

The mass of an element released in electroysis is proportional to the total charge passed.

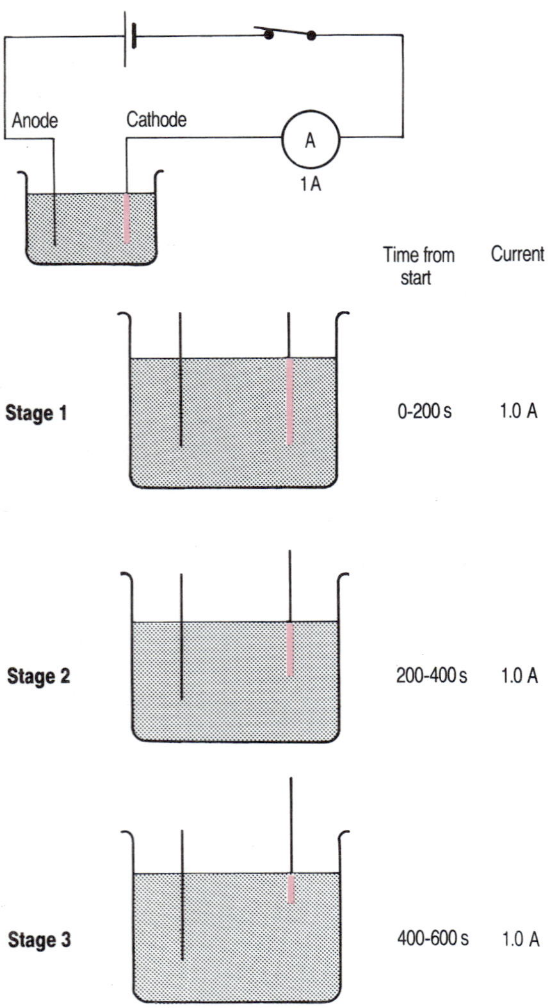

Questions

1 Use the graphs in Figure 3.6 to answer the following questions.
  a What mass of copper was deposited by a current of 2 A for 500 s?
  b What mass of copper was deposited by a current of 2.5 A for 400 s?
  c Why are your answers to **a** and **b** the same?

2 In Figure 3.5 the cathode was coated with copper on one side only. The area of this side was 42 cm^2.
  a What is the volume of a copper coating of thickness 0.01 cm on this plate?
  b Use the equation

$$\text{Density} = \frac{\text{mass}}{\text{volume}}$$

  to work out the mass of this volume of copper. The density of copper is 8.9 g/cm^3.
  c Work out the thickness of the mass of copper deposited in question **1a**.

3 Leroy and Mira used the apparatus shown in Figure 3.5 to investigate copper plating. They used the same plate at three different depths, as shown in Figure 3.9.
  a Work out the charge passed in each part of the experiment.
  b Which part of the cathode has the thickest coating and which part has the thinnest coating?
  c How does the thickness of the coating vary from the top to the bottom of the cathode?

4 A copper atom has a mass which is 63 times the mass of a hydrogen atom. Electrolysis experiments show that 31.5 g of copper and 1 g of hydrogen are released by the same amount of charge. What does this tell you about the charge of a copper ion compared with the charge of a hydrogen ion?

5 In the electrolysis of alumina to produce molten aluminium, 0.93 g of aluminium are produced for every 10 000 C of charged passed.
  a How much charge must be passed to produce 1 kg of aluminium?
  b How much current must be passed to produce 1 kg in 1 day?

3.3 Cells and batteries

Do you have a personal stereo? If so, you know that you can walk around outside with it because it is battery powered. It does not use mains electricity. Fortunately, it does not need too much electrical energy. If it did, it would need a much heavier battery. Carrying that around would be awkward.

Batteries are made in different shapes and sizes. A single battery should really be called an **electric cell**. Several cells connected together made up a **battery**. An electric cell produces electrical energy. Most cells contain chemicals that react together to produce electrical energy.

Rechargeable cells

If the circuit in Figure 3.10 is left switched on, the torch bulb eventually fades out completely. This happens because the zinc plate gradually dissolves in the acid and the acid becomes weaker and weaker. The cell **discharges** or 'runs down'. This cell is an example of a **primary** cell because it cannot be reused. Batteries that need to be replaced after use are made from primary cells.

Rechargeable cells and batteries can be discharged and recharged many times. When a rechargeable cell is charged up after use, the chemicals return to where they started. For example, when a car battery (see Figure 3.11) is used, lead plates dissolve in the battery acid. When the battery is recharged, the lead goes back on to the plates. This is an example of a **secondary** cell.

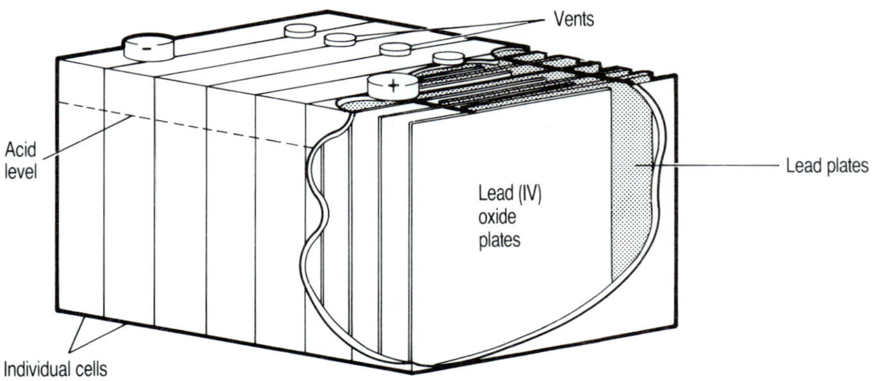

Figure 3.11 Inside a car battery

Battery voltage

A battery or cell in a circuit produces charge and pushes it, making it flow round the circuit. The higher the voltage of a battery, the more charge it can push round a circuit each second. Figure 3.13 shows how a **voltmeter** can be used to measure the voltage of a battery.

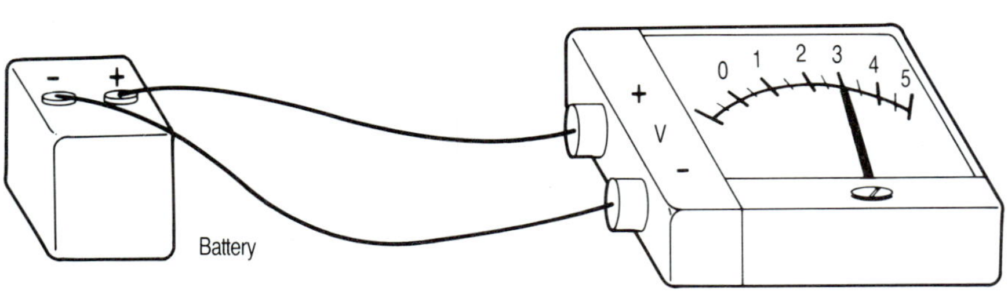

Figure 3.13 Measuring battery voltage

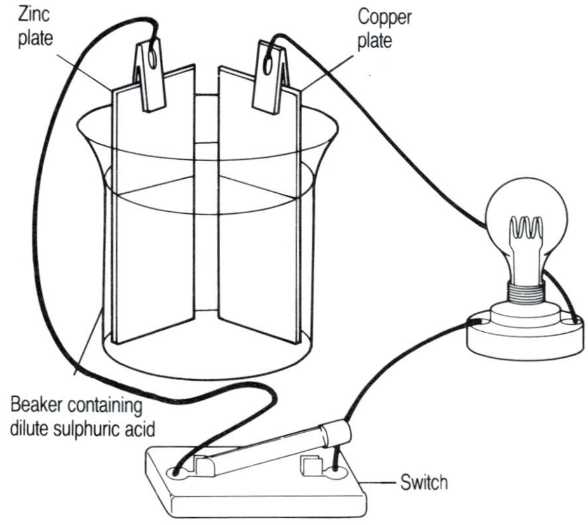

Figure 3.10 A simple cell

Activity 3.3

Testing a car battery

Cars are often difficult to start on cold mornings. If a car battery is in poor condition, the car may not start. This happens if the battery is not recharged. The battery acid (the electrolyte) becomes weaker and weaker if the battery is allowed to discharge.

The density of battery acid is a measure of the acid's strength. A **hydrometer** can be used to test the acid to see if the battery needs recharging.

- Test a car battery as shown in Figure 3.12.
- Does the battery need recharging?

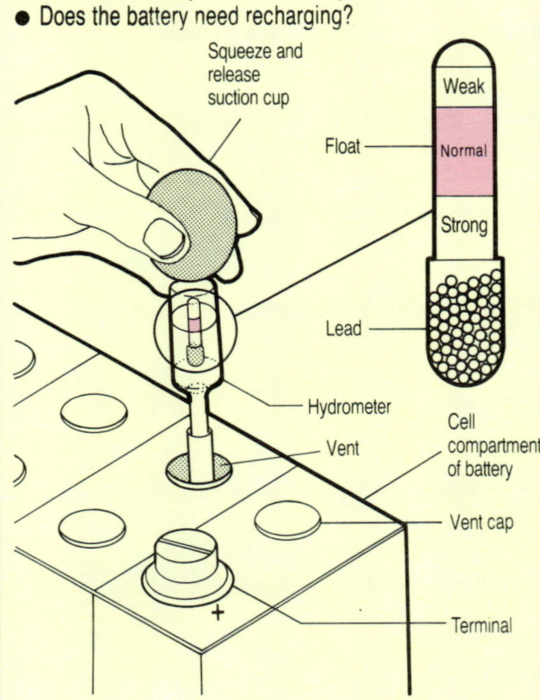

Figure 3.12 Using a hydrometer

In a circuit, charge from a cell transfers energy from the cell to the circuit components. Chemical reactions inside the cell force electrons on to one electrode (which becomes negative) and off the other electrode (which becomes positive). The electrons therefore gain **electrical potential energy**.

The electrons are forced to go round the circuit, releasing electrical potential energy on their journey. They re-enter the cell at its positive terminal and are resupplied with electrical energy before being pushed out at the negative terminal again.

The voltage of a battery or cell is called its **electromotive force**, usually shortened to **emf**. Measured in **volts**, emf is defined as the amount of electrical energy (in joules) produced for each coulomb of charge from the cell.

For example, a 12 V battery in a circuit produces 12 J of electrical energy for each coulomb of charge. In a circuit, the charge delivers this energy to the circuit's components.

The electrical energy produced by a battery can be worked out from the equation

$$\text{Electrical energy} = \text{voltage} \times \text{charge}$$

Worked example

A 12 V battery is used to light a 4 A car headlamp bulb for 30 minutes. Work out

a the charge delivered by the battery in this time

b the electrical energy produced by the battery.

Solution

a Charge (C) = current (A) × time (s)

= 4.0 × (30 × 60) = **7200 C**

b Battery emf = 12 V, so each coulomb of charge is supplied with 12 J of electrical energy by the battery.

Total electrical energy produced = emf (V) × charge (C)

= 12 × 7200

= **86 400 J**

Figure 3.14 A recharging unit in use

How efficient is a rechargeable battery?

When a battery is recharged, electrical energy from the recharging device is converted to chemical energy in the battery. After recharging, the battery can be used again to supply electrical energy.

- For every 100 J supplied to the battery during charging, how much is returned?

  Here is some data for a 9 V battery (see Figure 3.14).

  A 9 V recharging unit took 17 h to recharge the battery at a current of 0.01 A.

  a How much energy was supplied to the battery during recharging? The total charge pushed into the battery by the recharging unit can be worked out using:

  $$\text{Charge} = \text{current} \times \text{time} = 0.01 \times (17 \times 60 \times 60) = 612 \text{ C}$$

  At 9 V, each coulomb of charge supplied 9 J to the battery. The total energy supplied during recharging is given by:

  $$\text{Energy supplied} = \text{charge} \times \text{voltage} = 9 \times 612 = 5508 \text{ J}$$

  b In use, the 9 V battery can supply a steady current of 0.1 A for 1 h. Work out for yourself how much electrical energy the battery can produce. Then work out what percentage this is of the energy supplied during recharging.

Your results should show that the battery returns 59% of the electrical energy supplied to it. In other words, for every 100 J supplied to recharge it, the battery returns 59 J of electrical energy when used normally.

- What do you think happens to the rest of the energy?

Summary

A battery or a cell produces electrical energy. The emf of a cell is the amount of electrical energy produced per coulomb of charge. It is measured in volts. One volt equals 1 joule per coulomb.

Questions

1 An electric milk float is powered by a set of 12 V batteries. These are recharged in the milk depot after the float has been used to deliver milk.

a Describe the energy changes in the batteries when the float is 'on delivery'.

b What energy changes occur in the batteries when they are being recharged?

2 A heart pacemaker fitted inside a person's chest carries a small battery that is designed to last for at least five years. Yet a much larger battery in a torch lasts for less than a day in continuous use.

a Why is it important for a heart pacemaker to have a long-life battery?

b Why is the 'life' of a torch battery in normal use much shorter than that of a tiny pacemaker battery?

3 A 1.5 V cell supplies a current of 0.1 A to drive a cassette motor for 30 minutes. Work out

a the charge that passes through the motor in this time

b the electrical energy produced by the battery in this time.

4 A car has an **alternator** that charges up the car battery. This is a generator driven by the car engine.

a What energy changes occur when an alternator is used to charge a car battery?

b A car is parked and left with its lights on. The driver returns after a few hours and has difficulty starting the engine. Why?

5 Design a system to light an LED if the strength of acid in a car battery falls below a certain value.

Unit 4
Electric circuits

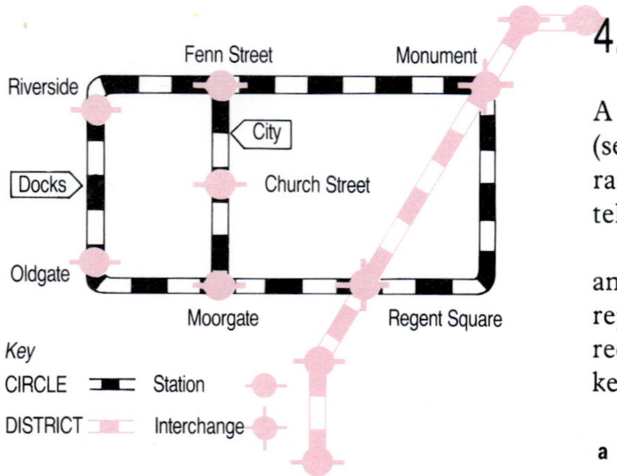

Figure 4.1 A rail map is like a circuit diagram

4.1 Loops and junctions

A circuit diagram can be a bit like a map of an underground rail system (see Figure 4.1). Stations, lines, branches and junctions form a network of rail links under the streets. Maps of the network usually include a key to tell the reader what the symbols represent.

Circuit diagrams also use standard symbols. Unlike the network maps of an underground, you have to remember which component each symbol represents. Figure 4.2 shows some common electrical symbols. Can you recognise them all? You might get lost beyond this point if you can't. The key is on page 79.

Figure 4.2 Electrical symbols

Activity 4.1

Torch circuits

Figure 4.3 shows a cut-away diagram of a torch. In electrical terms, it consists of two 1.5 V cells, a 3 V torch bulb and a switch.

- Which one of the circuit diagrams in Figure 4.4 represents the torch circuit? Make up each circuit to find out which diagram is correct.

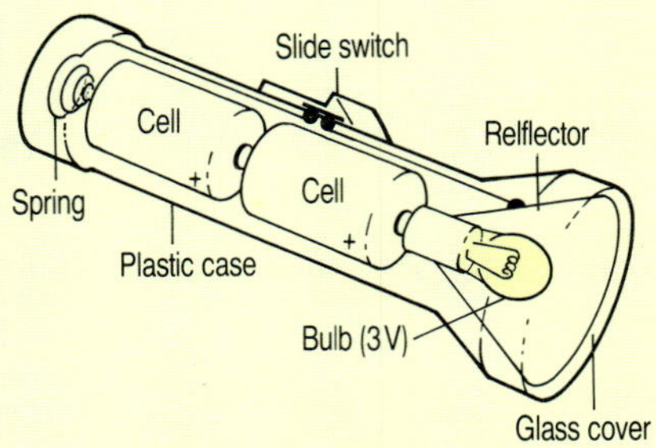

Figure 4.3 Inside a torch

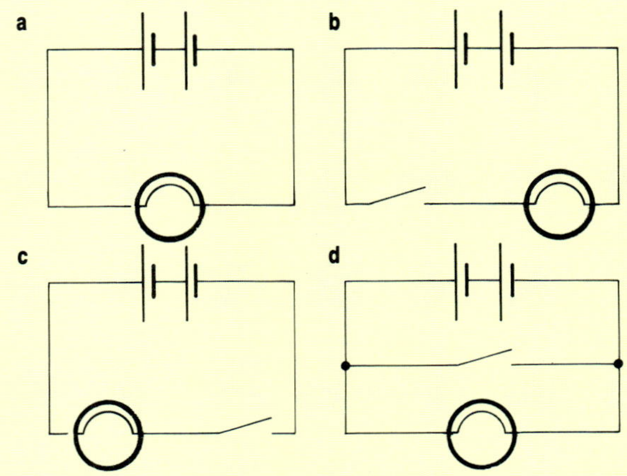

Figure 4.4 Which diagram represents the torch circuit?

A current problem

Sean and Emma have wired up circuit **a** of Figure 4.4. Sean claims that the current leaving the torch bulb is less than the current entering it. 'The bulb uses up current', he says.

To convince Emma, he decides to connect a second bulb into the circuit, as in Figure 4.5. 'The second bulb will not be as bright because the first one uses up most of the current', he says. He tries the test and finds that *both* bulbs are now dim.

- Why was his prediction wrong?

Emma suggests using ammeters to investigate the circuits. She tests the circuits as follows.

Test 1: She wires up circuit **a** of Figure 4.6. The two ammeters show the same reading. The current leaving the torch bulb is the same as the current entering the torch bulb.

Test 2: She makes circuit **b** of Figure 4.6. The ammeters again read the same. However, the reading is less than with circuit **a**. The cell voltage is shared between the two bulbs.

The two bulbs in circuit **b** are **in series** with each other. The same current passes through them both. If one bulb is unscrewed from its holder, the other bulb goes off too.

Each circuit in Figure 4.6 is a single loop. In each circuit, the cell pushes current round the loop from the postive terminal of the cell to the negative terminal. The current is the same at any point in the loop. An ammeter connected in series with a cell and other components gives the same reading wherever it is connected.

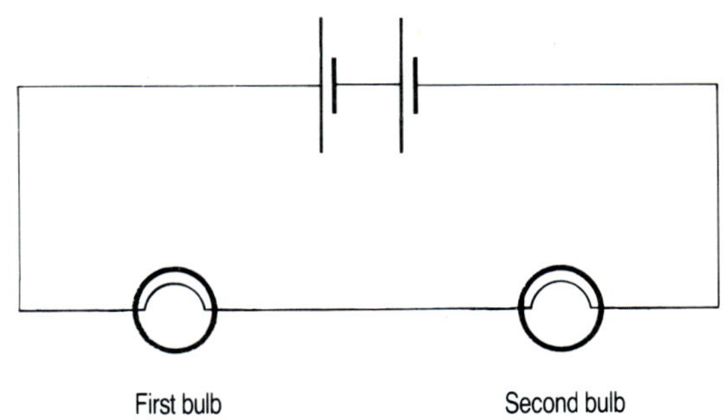

Figure 4.5 A current problem

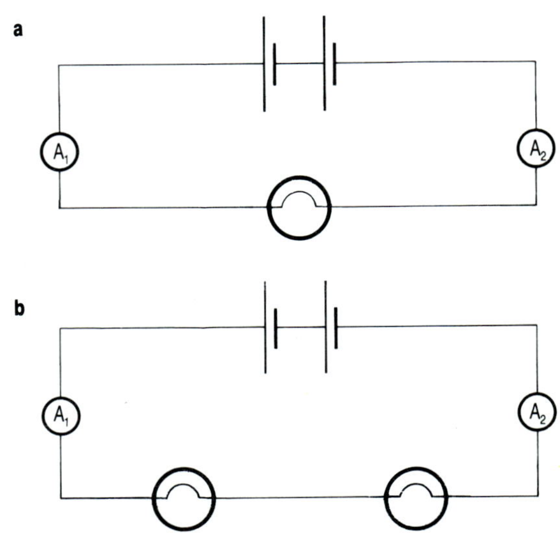

Figure 4.6 Using ammeters

Measuring current without an ammeter

To measure current with an ammeter, you have to connect the ammeter into the circuit. Figure 4.8 shows how a plotting compass can be used instead of an ammeter. The plotting compass is not part of the circuit.

1. Place the plotting compass under the connecting wire at different points around the circuit. Find a point where the compass deflects about 45° when the current is switched on.
2. Change the current in the circuit and see what happens to the deflection of the compass.

This experiment was first carried out by André Ampere over 150 years ago. His discoveries about electric current were so important that the unit of current, the **ampere**, is named after him.

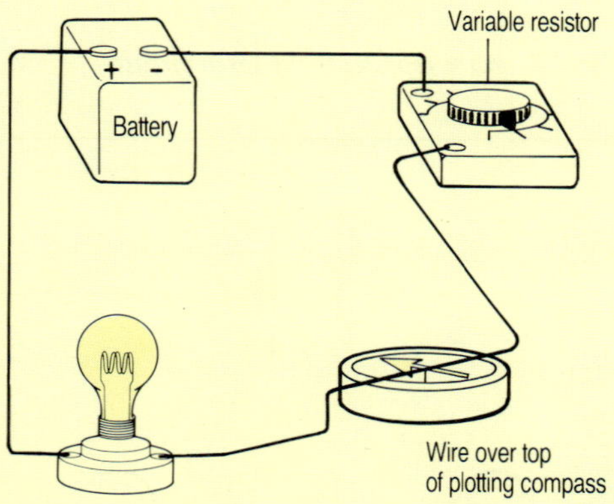

Figure 4.8 Using a plotting compass

Components in parallel

At home, you can turn each light bulb on or off using a switch in series with the bulb. Switching a light bulb on or off does not affect any other light bulb. This is because the light bulbs are connected **in parallel** with each other.

Figure 4.7 shows a circuit with two torch bulbs in parallel with each other. The circuit has more than one loop. An ammeter is used to measure the current through each bulb. The result of closing different switches is shown in Table 4.1.

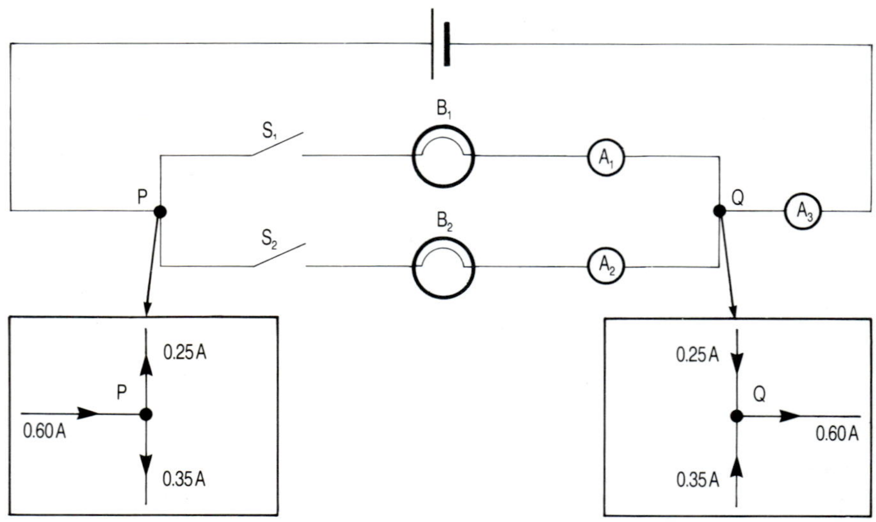

Figure 4.7 Bulbs in parallel

Switches		**Bulbs**		**Ammeter readings** (A)		
$\mathbf{S_1}$	$\mathbf{S_2}$	$\mathbf{B_1}$	$\mathbf{B_2}$	$\mathbf{A_1}$	$\mathbf{A_2}$	$\mathbf{A_3}$
Closed	Open	ON	OFF	0.25	0.00	0.25
Open	Closed	OFF	ON	0.00	0.35	0.35
Closed	Closed	ON	ON	0.25	0.35	0.60

Table 4.1

Can you see the link between the ammeter readings? In the last case, the cell current is 0.6 A. The cell current is equal to the sum of the currents through each bulb.

With both switches closed, the current leaving junction Q is 0.6 A. The current entering junction Q is 0.25 A through ammeter A_1 and 0.35 A through ammeter A_2. The circuit obeys a law called *Kirchoff's First Law.* It says that the total current entering a junction equals the total current leaving it.

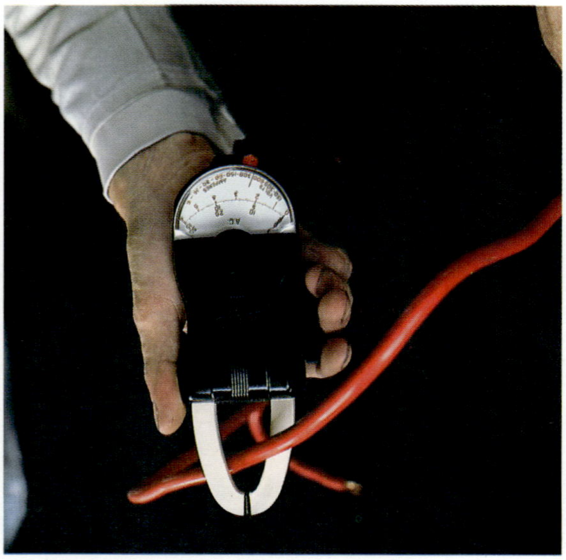

Figure 4.9 A clampmeter

The clampmeter

A **clampmeter** (see Figure 4.9) is a modern version of the plotting compass ammeter. It clips on to a cable to measure the current passing along it. Electrical engineers use clampmeters to measure currents up to 1000 A.

A car lighting circuit

A car has several sets of light bulbs including headlights, tail lights and brake lights. Figure 4.10 shows the circuit diagram for these three sets of lights. An ammeter inside the car shows the current entering this circuit. Figure 4.10 gives the current taken by each bulb. For each set of lights, the current taken is therefore:
Headlights only – 8 A
Tail lights only – 3.6 A
Brake lights only – 1 A.

- What is the ammeter reading when the headlights *and* tail lights only are on?
  The current through the ammeter splits into 8 A through the headlights and 3.6 A through the tail lights. The ammeter reading is therefore 8 + 3.6 = 11.6 A.
- What is the reading when all three sets of lights are on?

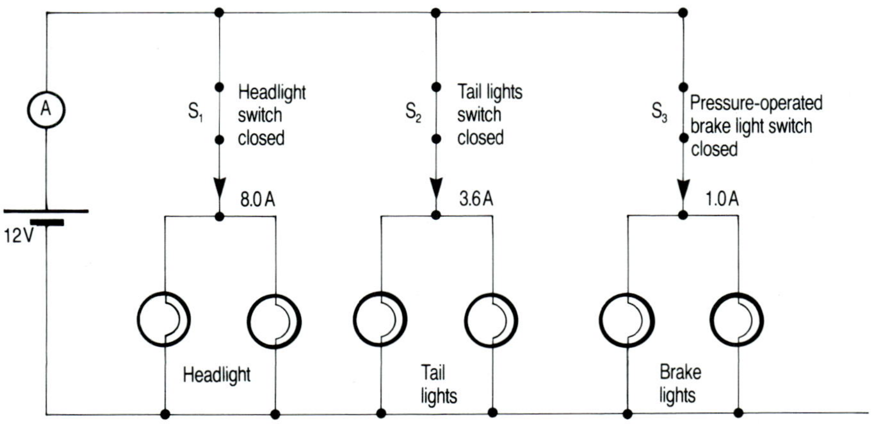

Figure 4.10 Car lighting circuit

A circuit model

An electric circuit is a bit like a central heating system. The battery in an electric circuit pushes charge around the circuit. The pump in a central heating system pushes water around the system. The water current is the rate of flow of water. The electric current is the rate of flow of charge.

Figure 4.11 shows a central heating system similar to the electric circuit in Figure 4.10. A stop valve is used to control the flow to the living room radiators. This is a bit like the switch in Figure 4.10 used to turn the headlights and tail lights on or off. However, the stop valve is not an on/off device. Which electrical component in Figure 4.2 is it like?

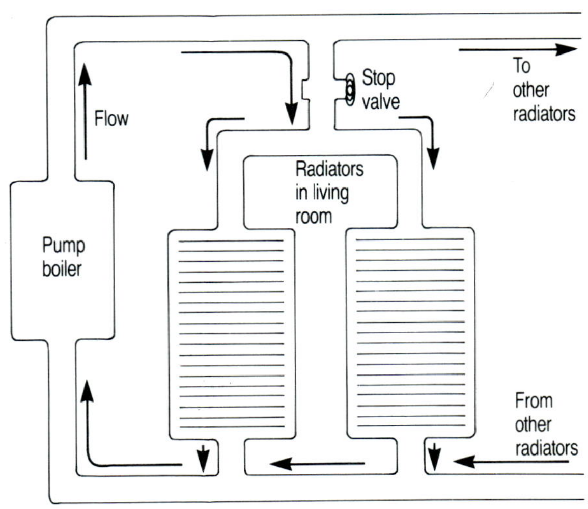

Figure 4.11 A central heating system (compare this with Figure 4.10)

Summary

Current is measured in amperes using an ammeter. Components in series pass the same current. At a junction, the total current entering the junction is equal to the total current leaving it.

Questions

1 Look at the rail network in Figure 4.1. Trains on the Circle line travelling clockwise go along either the City branch or the Docks branch.
 a Are these two branches in series or in parallel?
 b Six trains per hour pass clockwise through Moorgate station. Two trains per hour pass clockwise through Church Street station. How many trains per hour pass clockwise through the Docks branch?
2 A third torch bulb and switch are added to the circuit of Figure 4.7 so that each bulb can be switched on or off independently.
 a Sketch the new circuit diagram.
 b When all three switches are closed, the ammeter reads 0.85 A. How much current passes through the third torch bulb?
3 Amy wants to make a circuit with four identical torch bulbs in parallel, connected to a 1.5 V cell which is in series with a variable resistor. Each torch bulb is marked '1.5 V, 250 mA'.
 a Sketch the circuit diagram.
 b What will be the maximum current from the cell in this circuit?
4 In Figure 4.10, the ammeter scale reads from zero to 20 A. Sketch the ammeter scale and mark on it the needle's position when
 a the headlights and tail lights are on
 b all three sets of lights are on
 c all three sets of lights are on except for one of the headlights.
5 Design a system based on Figure 4.10 to show, on the ammeter, if any of the light bulbs have failed.

4.2 Potential difference

When a torch lamp is switched on, chemical energy from the cell is converted to electrical energy. The torch bulb converts electrical energy from the cell into heat and light energy.

The amount of electrical energy produced per coulomb of charge inside the cell is the **emf** of the cell. So a 1.5 V cell that pushes 100 coulombs of charge through a torch bulb produces $1.5 \times 100 = 150$ J of electrical energy.

- What happens to this energy?

Most of it is converted to heat and light in the torch bulb, and some is converted to heat inside the cell or in the wires. If the cell is used to drive a motor, some of the electrical energy it produces is changed to kinetic energy in the motor.

Suppose the cell is connected in series with a torch bulb and a motor, as in Figure 4.12. Some of the electrical energy from the cell is delivered to the torch bulb and some to the motor. Assuming no energy is wasted as heat in the cell or in the wires, the energy from the cell equals the energy delivered to the motor and torch bulb:

$$\text{Electrical energy produced by cell} = \text{electrical energy delivered to bulb} + \text{electrical energy delivered to motor}$$

The **potential difference** or 'voltage' across a component in a circuit is the amount of electrical energy per coulomb of charge *delivered* to the component. Potential difference, or pd, is measured in volts. One volt is 1 joule per coulomb.

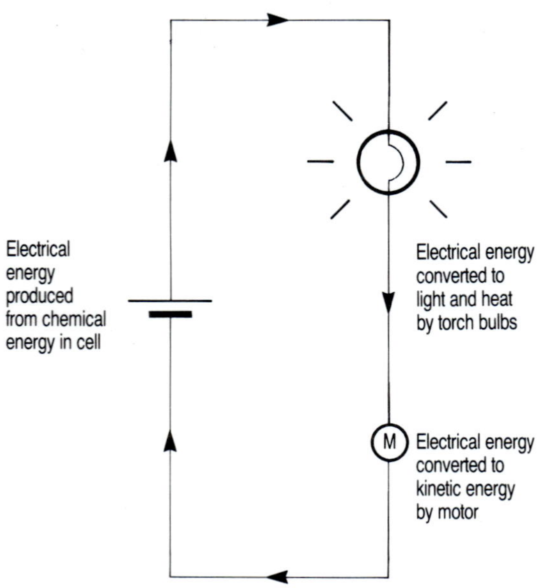

Figure 4.12 Electrical energy

Activity 4.3

Measuring voltages

A **voltmeter** is used to measure potential difference. Figure 4.13 shows how voltmeters can be used to measure the pd across torch bulbs connected to a cell. Table 4.2 shows that the reading of each voltmeter is equal to the amount of electrical energy delivered to the torch bulb by each coulomb of charge that passes through it.

Reading	Energy delivered
V_1 = 1.0 V	To X: 1.0 J/C
V_2 = 0.5 V	To Y: 0.5 J/C

Table 4.2

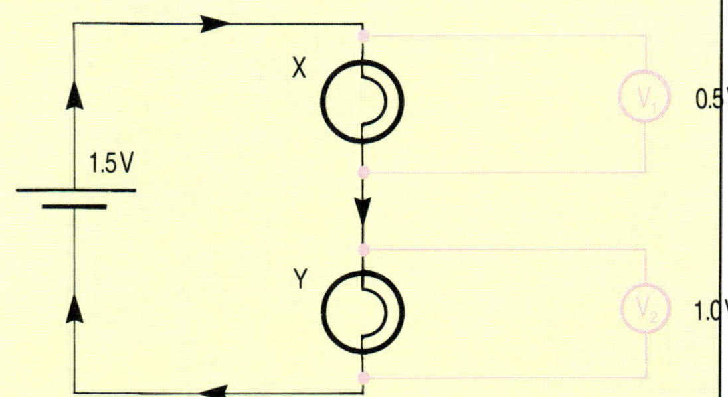

Figure 4.13 Using voltmeters

Figure 4.14 shows a torch bulb in series with a variable resistor and a cell.

- How does the pd across the torch bulb change as the variable resistor is adjusted?

Two sets of readings are shown in Table 4.3.

1 Set up the circuit.
2 Copy Table 4.3 and add your own headings to it.

At normal brightness, no electrical energy is delivered to the variable resistor because V_2 = 0. Each coulomb of charge passing through the torch bulb delivers 1.5 J to the bulb from the cell.

When the torch bulb is very dim, each coulomb of charge from the cell delivers 0.5 J to the bulb and 1 J to the variable resistor. The electrical energy from the cell (1.5 J/C) is shared between the torch bulb and the variable resistor. This is why the voltmeter readings add up to 1.5 V.

Your results should show that for two components in series, as in Figure 4.14,

$$\text{Total pd, } V, = V_1 + V_2$$

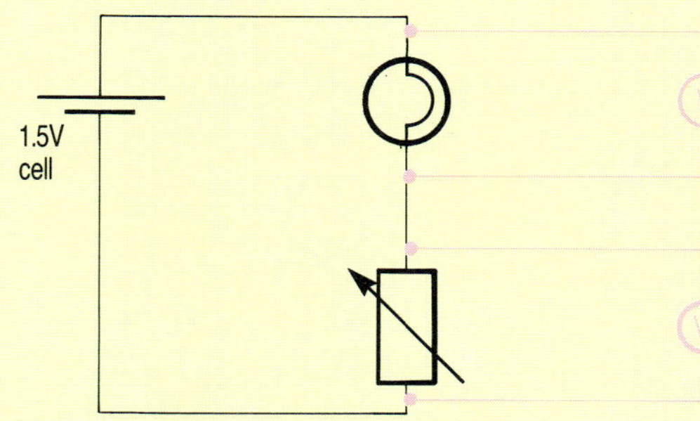

Figure 4.14 Components in series

Torch bulb	Voltmeter readings (V)	
	V_1	V_2
Normal brightness	1.5	0.0
Dim	0.9	0.6
Very dim	0.5	1.0

Table 4.3

An energy puzzle

Graham and Catherine have connected up the circuit in Figure 4.15 which contains two torch bulbs in parallel. Catherine measures the pd across each bulb and across the dimmer, as follows, keeping the dimmer fixed.

1 Pd across bulb A = 1.2 V
2 Pd across bulb B = 1.2 V
3 Pd across dimmer = 0.3 V

'That means the total pd is 2.7 V. If I connect a voltmeter across the cell, it should read 2.7 V', she claims.

However, when she does this, the voltmeter reads 1.5 V. Catherine reckons this is because the bulbs are in parallel, not in series.

Each coulomb of charge from the cell passes *either* through A *or* through B – not through both. Therefore each coulomb of charge delivers 1.2 J to A *or* B and 0.3 J to the dimmer. So the total energy delivered per coulomb is 1.5 J. This is why the voltmeter reading across the cell is 1.5 V (= 1.5 J/C).

Graham predicts that if the pd across the dimmer is increased to 0.8 V, the pd across each bulb will be 0.7 V. Why?

These results show that two components in parallel have the same pd.

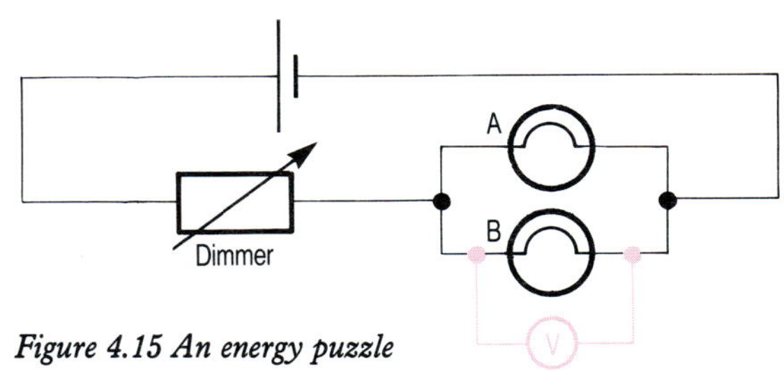

Figure 4.15 An energy puzzle

Circuit training

Do you like to keep fit? Figure 4.16 shows a keep-fit circuit. You start by climbing the ladder on to a platform, from where you either slide down a rope to the ground, or you jump. Whichever route you choose to descend, you lose the same amount of potential energy. The two routes are in parallel with each other.

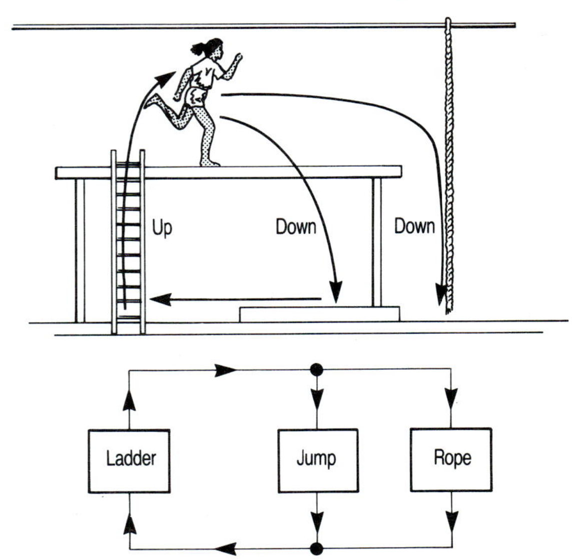

Figure 4.16 Circuit training

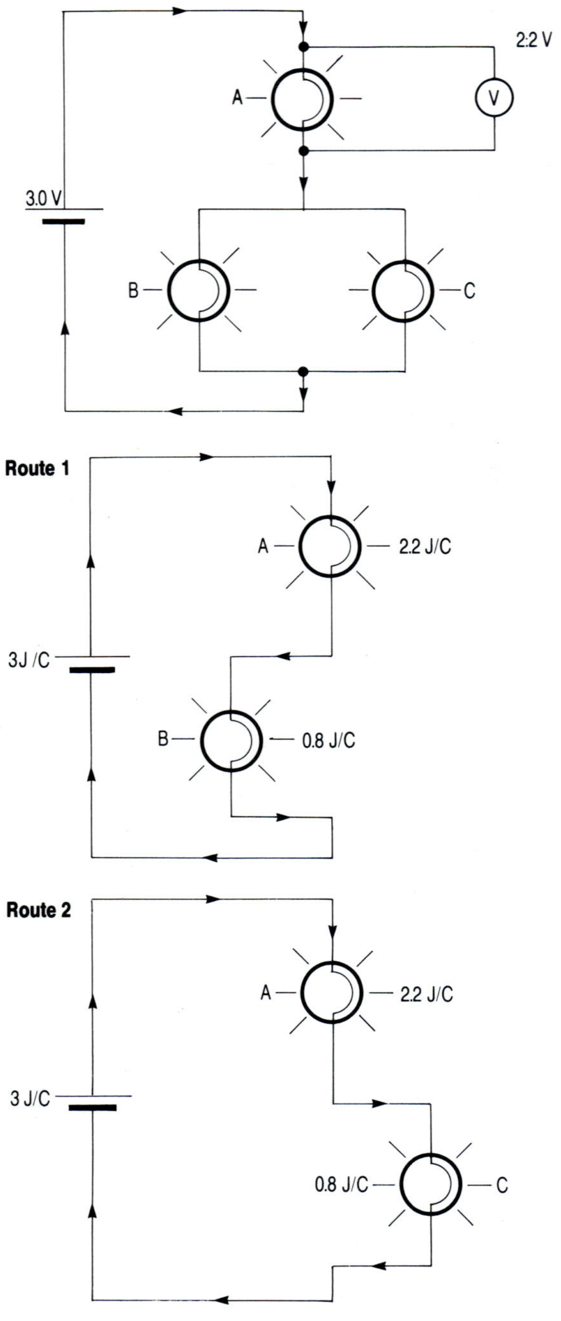

Figure 4.17 Circuit routes

Suppose you gain 4000 J of potential energy each time you climb the ladder. This energy is released whichever route you choose to come down. For each trip round, you release 4000 J of potential energy. The potential energy released equals the potential energy gained.

In an electric circuit, charge flows round the circuit. Electrical energy is produced in the cells of the circuit. This energy is delivered to the components of the circuit.

Figure 4.17 shows the energy flow in a circuit with a single cell and three torch bulbs. The emf of the cell is 3 V, so each coulomb of charge from the cell has 3 J of electrical energy.

● Where does this energy go to?

Route 1: Charge can flow around the circuit via bulbs A and B. The voltmeter across A reads 2.2 V. Therefore each coulomb of charge gives up 2.2 J on passing through A and 0.8 J on passing through B.

Route 2: Charge can flow via bulb C instead of bulb B. Each coulomb gives up 0.8 J whether it goes through B or through C.

For both routes, the electrical energy delivered to the components is equal to the electrical energy produced in the cell. The cell supplies electrical energy to the circuit and the components take the energy out of the circuit.

Summary

The potential difference or voltage across a component is the electrical energy delivered per coulomb of charge to the component. In a circuit, the electrical energy produced is equal to the electrical energy delivered.

Questions

1 In Figure 4.14, when the torch bulb is dim, voltmeter V_1 reads 0.9 V and voltmeter V_2 reads 0.6 V. For each coulomb of charge flowing round the circuit,
- **a** how much electrical energy is delivered to each bulb?
- **b** how much electrical energy is produced by the cell?

2 The emf of the cell shown in Figure 4.15 is 1.5 V.
- **a** When the pd across the dimmer is 0.5 V, what is the pd across each bulb?
- **b** The dimmer is adjusted to make the pd across each component the same. What is the pd across each bulb now?

3 Rubinda connects two torch bulbs and dimmers to a 6 V battery, as in Figure 4.18. One torch bulb is marked '3.5 V, 400 mA' and the other is marked '2.5 V, 250 mA'. Each dimmer is adjusted so that the bulb it controls lights at normal brightness. The pd and current for each bulb is then as marked on the bulbs.
- **a** What is the current through **i** each bulb **ii** the cell?
- **b** What is the pd across **i** each bulb **ii** each dimmer?

4 The torch bulbs in question **3** and **one** of the dimmers are reconnected in series with the 6 V battery and an ammeter.
- **a** Sketch the circuit diagram.
- **b** The dimmer is adjusted until the 2.5 V torch bulb lights at normal brightness. What is the current through each component?
- **c** A voltmeter is connected across the dimmer and reads 0.8 V when the 2.5 V torch bulb is at normal brightness. What is the pd across the other torch bulb?

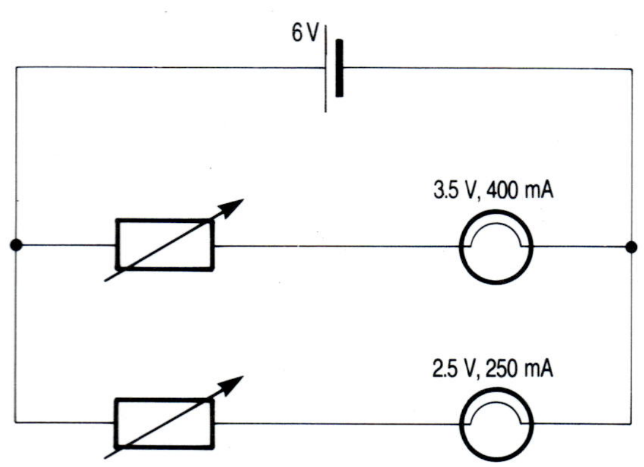

Figure 4.18

Unit 5

Electricity in the home

5.1 Electrical power

Here are some uses for electricity:

- listening to a radio – creating sound waves
- cooking a meal – heating food
- working a lift – moving upwards
- heating our homes – keeping warm
- pumping water to our homes – moving water through pipes
- chatting over the phone – sending information.

The jobs involve either moving or heating things. Figure 5.1 shows some more uses for electricity. Can you think of a use for electricity that does not involve moving or heating something?

Figure 5.1 Electricity powers all these appliances

Energy on the move

Before electricity was first supplied to homes, coal was the main source of fuel for heating. Smoke from coal fires in homes caused a great deal of air pollution which affected the health of millions of people.

Nowadays, we can keep warm in winter using electricity generated in coal-fired power stations. These power stations are fitted with equipment to remove smoke and dust from the waste gases. Coal is still burned – but mostly in power stations, not in homes.

Until about 1960, most trains were steam powered. They burned coal, adding to the smoke from homes. Electric trains are now used instead (see Figure 5.2). Their energy is supplied through electric cables or rails. These trains are cleaner and much more efficient than steam trains.

Figure 5.2 Power without smoke

Measuring electrical energy

In an electric circuit, energy is 'on the move' as charge flows around the circuit. A **joulemeter** is an instrument that measures electrical energy. Figure 5.3 shows a joulemeter being used to measure the energy supplied to a lamp bulb.

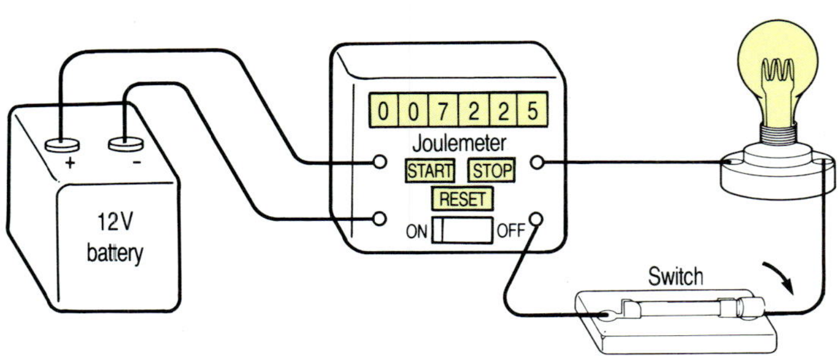

Figure 5.3 Measuring electrical energy

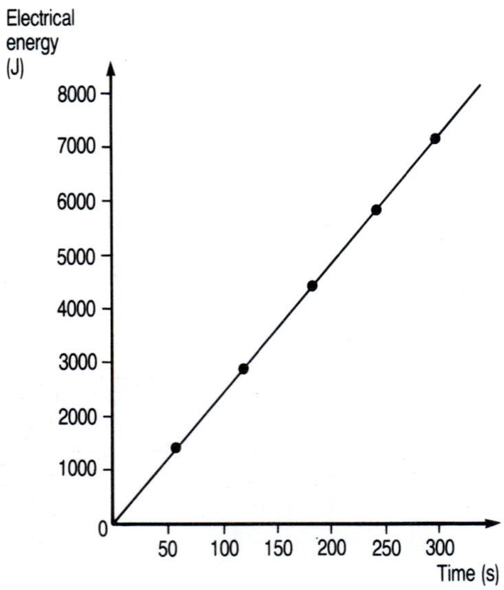

Figure 5.4 Graph of electrical energy against time

- When the switch is open, the bulb is off and the joulemeter reading does not change – because no electrical energy is being used by the bulb.
- When the switch is closed, the bulb lights up and the joulemeter reading increases at a steady rate. Its reading every 60 s after closing the switch is as shown in Table 5.1.

Time (s)	0	60	120	180	240	300
Reading (J)	0	1445	2905	4350	5805	7225

Table 5.1

These measurements are plotted on a graph, as shown in Figure 5.4. Read off from the graph how many joules are used in 100 s. Then work out how many joules are used each second. You should get an answer of 24 J/s.

Power

The electrical energy used each second by a device is the **power** supplied to it. Power is energy used per second. It is measured in **watts** (W). One watt equals 1 J/s. In the above example, the bulb uses 24 J of electrical energy each second.

Power supplied = electrical energy used per second

In Figure 5.3, the bulb can be replaced by other devices to measure the power supplied to them. Here are some results for different devices:

A 3 V electric motor from a personal stereo used 150 J in 100 s
A 12 V heater used 1000 J in 20 s
A 6 V torch bulb used 18 J in 50 s

- Which one used the most power?

The heater used 50 J/s (= 1000 J/20 s) so the power supplied was 50 W.

- Did the heater take more power than the other devices?

Work out the power supplied to the motor and bulb.

The **power rating** of an electrical device is the electrical power it takes in normal use. For example, a light bulb marked '240 V, 60 W' takes 60 J of electrical energy each second in normal use.

The electrical power equation

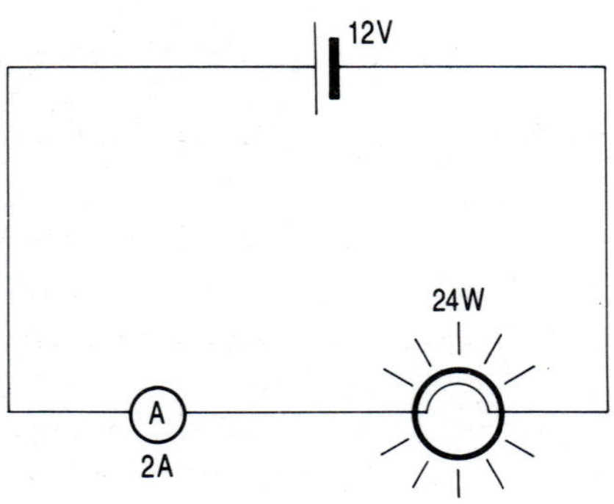

Figure 5.5 Working out power

In Figure 5.5, a 12 V battery is connected to a light bulb in series with an ammeter. The ammeter reads 2 A. This means that 2 coulombs of charge pass through the bulb each second (since charge = current × time).

The voltage across the bulb is 12 V. Each coulomb of charge passing through the bulb delivers 12 J of electrical energy to the bulb (since 1 volt = 1 J/C).

- How much energy is supplied to the bulb each second?

Two coulombs of charge deliver 24 J. Therefore the power supplied to the bulb is 24 W (= 24 J/s). In other words, since

$$\text{Current} = \frac{\text{charge}}{\text{time}}$$

and

$$\text{Voltage} = \frac{\text{energy}}{\text{charge}}$$

then $$\text{Current} \times \text{voltage} = \frac{\text{charge}}{\text{time}} \times \frac{\text{energy}}{\text{charge}} = \frac{\text{energy}}{\text{time}} = \text{power}$$

Electrical power can be worked out from current and voltage using this equation:

$$\underset{(\text{W})}{\text{Electrical power}} = \underset{(\text{A})}{\text{current}} \times \underset{(\text{V})}{\text{voltage}}$$

Working out fuse ratings

When fitting a plug, you have to make sure you use the correct fuse. The fuse is there to protect an appliance from too much current, so it is dangerous to fit the wrong one. For example, Megan's fan heater normally takes a current of 4.2 A on full power. She fits a 5 A fuse to its plug. This allows the heater to operate at full power.

It would be dangerous if she had chosen a 13 A fuse for this heater. Suppose a fault develops in the heater and the current goes up to 10 A. The 13 A fuse would not blow. The heater would become very hot and could possibly start a fire. The 5 A fuse would have blown and cut the current off.

Megan worked out the correct rating for a fuse (ie the maximum current it can pass) from the power rating of the appliance. Megan's fan heater is marked '240 V, 1000 W'. She calculated the current it takes from:

$$\text{Power} = \text{current} \times \text{voltage}$$

so

$$1000\text{ W} = \text{current} \times 240\text{ V}$$

giving

$$\text{Current} = \frac{1000\text{ W}}{240\text{ V}} = 4.2\text{ A}$$

So the 5 A fuse allows the heater to operate at full power, and prevents the current rising above 5 A.

Summary

Power supplied is energy used per second. One watt of power equals 1 J/s. The current taken by an appliance can be worked out from the equation power = current × voltage.

Questions

1 Craig used a joulemeter to measure the electrical energy supplied to a 12 V heater. He took readings every 60 seconds. His results are shown in Table 5.3.
  a Plot a graph of the electrical energy used (vertical axis) against time.
  b Read off from your graph the energy used in 100 s.
  c How much energy would have been used in 1000 s?
  d What was the power supplied to the heater?

2 A torch bulb is marked '3 V, 0.25 A'. It is connected to a 3 V battery. Work out
  a the power supplied to the torch bulb
  b the electrical energy delivered in 300 s.

3 Josie needs to buy a fuse for an electric kettle. The kettle is marked '240 V, 2400 W'.
  a Work out the current taken by the appliance.
  b The shop stocks 3 A, 5 A nd 13 A fuses only. Which fuse should Josie buy?

4 An electric train operates from a live rail at 750 V. The motors that drive the train use up to 3750 kW of electrical power.
  a Work out the maximum current taken by the train's motors.
  b When the train is climbing a slope it uses more current than when it is descending the slope. Why?

5 Devise an experiment to check the accuracy of a joulemeter. You are given a light bulb that takes a current of 2 A at 12 V. List the apparatus you would use. Describe, with a diagram, how you would use it.

Activity 5.1

Checking power ratings

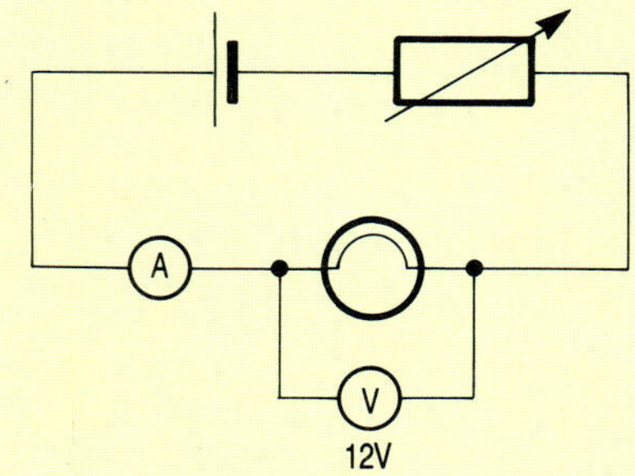

Figure 5.6 Checking power ratings

Steve wants to check the power ratings of two 12 V headlight bulbs. He wires up the circuit shown in Figure 5.6 and connects each bulb in turn into the circuit. Each time, he adjusts the variable resistor until the voltmeter reads 12 V. Then he records the ammeter reading. His readings are shown in Table 5.2.

Bulb marking	1 12 V, 55 W	2 12 V, 60 W
Ammeter reading (A)	4.6	4.8

Table 5.2

The power supplied to the first bulb is 12 V × 4.6 A = 55.2 W.

- Work out the power supplied to the second bulb.
- Which bulb's power rating is closest to Steve's results?

Time (s)	0	60	120	180	240	300
Reading (J)	0	2950	6010	8980	12 050	14 995

Table 5.3

19 November 1878

Floodlit Football – A Brilliant Success!

Supporters of Blackburn Rovers and Accrington will remember yesterday after being treated to one of the first floodlit matches in Britain. Six thousand fans paid to enter the ground and a further twenty thousand watched from Coronation Park.

The players, attired in picturesque costumes, amused the crowds before the match by playing leapfrog and racing. The leather, which was painted white so the players could see it, was kicked off at about a quarter to eight. Although the players' faces could not be distinguished at a distance, the ball could be seen very well and the crowd had no difficulty in following the match. Blackburn had a resounding victory – three goals to nil.

5.2 Home circuits

Have you had a power cut recently? If so you will have realised how much we depend on electricity – without it there is no electric light, no television, no washing machine, no fridge, no computer, etc. Homes were first connected up to the electricity mains about 80 years ago. Within 20 years most homes were wired up.

Electricity enters your home through an **electricity meter** and a **distribution box**. Separate circuits for heating and lighting branch off from the distribution box. Figure 5.7 shows the outline of the circuits.

Each circuit includes a **live** wire which is at 240 volts and a **neutral** wire which is at zero volts. The neutral wire is connected to the ground (ie earthed) in the electricity power station.

The master switch near the distribution box is used to disconnect the circuits from the electricity supply. This switch turns everything electrical in your home off.

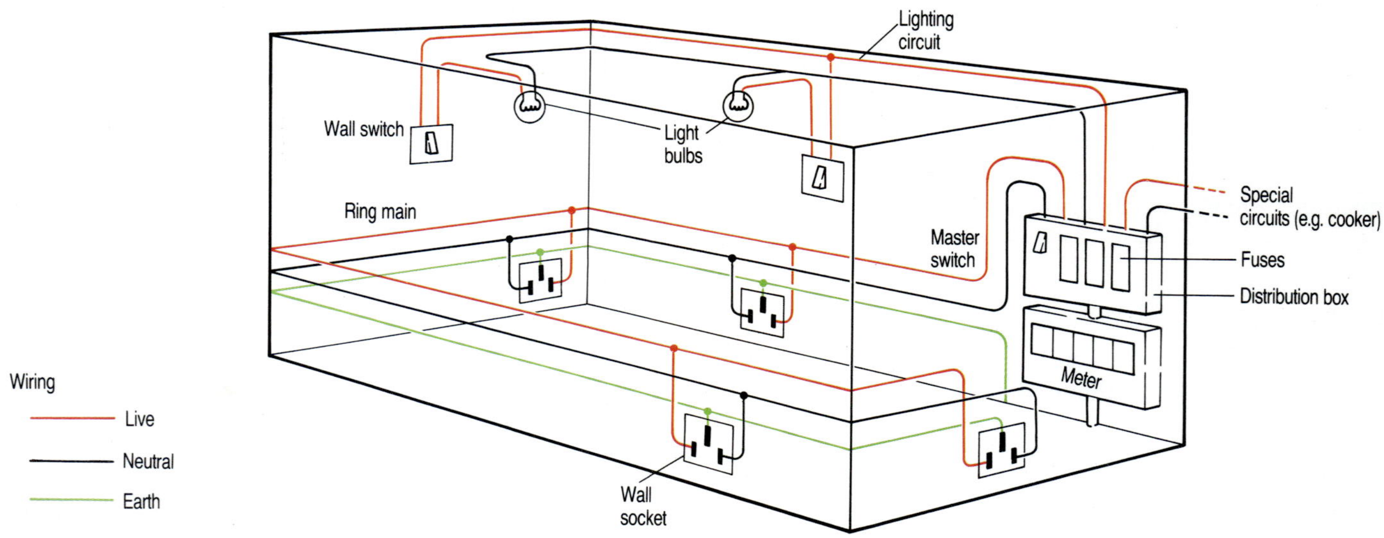

Figure 5.7 Home circuits

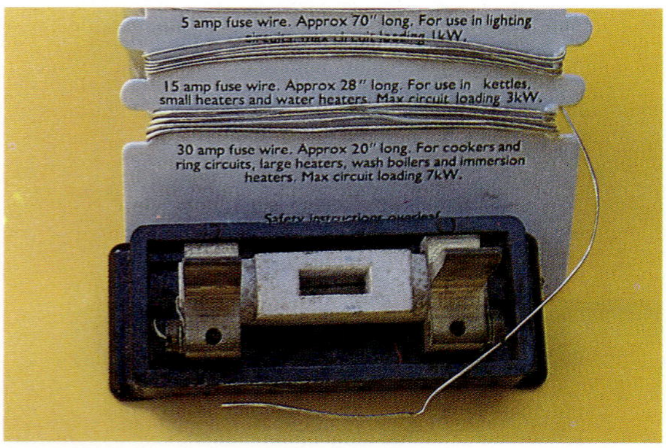

Figure 5.8 A rewireable fuse. Sometimes cartridge fuses are used instead

Fuses

A **fuse** contains a wire that melts if too much current passes through it. Figure 5.8 shows different types of fuse wire. A fuse blows if there is a fault, either in the wiring or in an appliance. For example, if the wires inside a table lamp touch where they are bare, current 'short-circuits' through the contact. This blows the fuse in the plug, cutting the current off.

The distribution box contains a fuse for each circuit in your home. This is to prevent too much current passing through the wires of the circuits. Too much current makes the fuse blow which causes a gap in the circuit. Modern distribution boxes are fitted with cartridge fuses. Rewireable fuses are found in older homes.

Every plug fitted to an electric appliance contains a cartridge fuse. This is to prevent too much current passing through the appliance if it develops a fault.

The ring main circuit

Each wall socket at home is part of a circuit called a **ring main**. This circuit includes an **earth** wire as well as the live and neutral wires. The earth wire is used to connect the case of an appliance to the ground. This is to prevent the case becoming live if a fault occurs in the appliance. If the case was not earthed and it became live, anyone touching it would be electrocuted.

The three pins of a three-pin plug (see Figure 5.9) connect to the live, neutral and earth wires of the ring main. The longest pin of a three-pin plug is the **earth** pin. The fuse inside the plug is connected directly to the **live** pin. The other pin is the **neutral** pin. The live terminal is at 240 V. The other terminals are at 0 V. The wires of a mains cable are colour coded, as shown in Figure 5.7. This is to ensure that each wire is connected to the correct pin when a plug is fitted to the cable.

Figure 5.9 A three-pin plug

Special circuits

Electric cookers and showers use much more power than most other appliances. For example, with the oven and all the rings of an electric cooker fully on, the total power used could be as much as 10 kW.

- What current is needed to supply 10 kW of power at 240 V?

The wires of the cooker circuit must be capable of carrying this amount of current without getting warm. That is why they are much thicker than ring main or lighting circuit wires (see Figure 5.10).

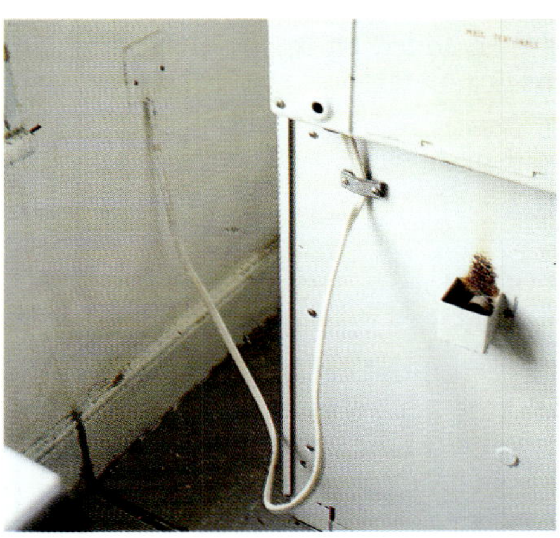

Figure 5.10 A special circuit

Activity 5.2

Make a model lighting circuit

1 Use torch bulbs and switches to make the circuit shown in Figure 5.11. One terminal of the cell is earthed to make one of the wires from the cell neutral. The other wire is live.

2 Open and close each switch to make sure each bulb works separately. The bulbs are in parallel with each other. Notice that the switches are on the live side of the bulbs. Why?

3 Close all the switches. The bulbs should all light up. The fuse wire might be warm, but it should not melt.

- Suppose one of the bulbs becomes faulty and current short-circuits between the live and the neutral wire. What do you think will happen?

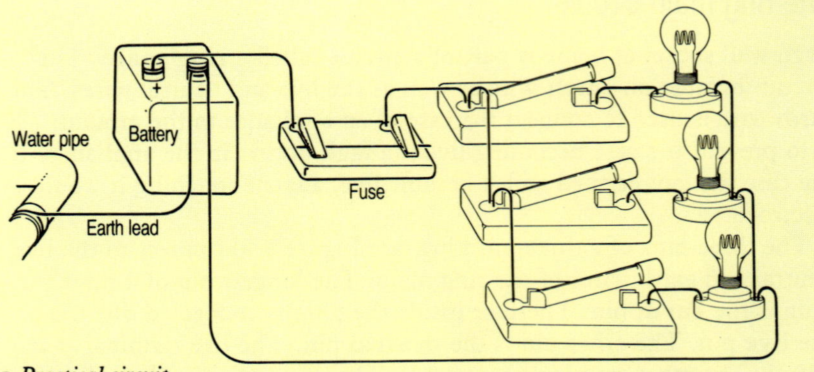

a *Practical circuit*

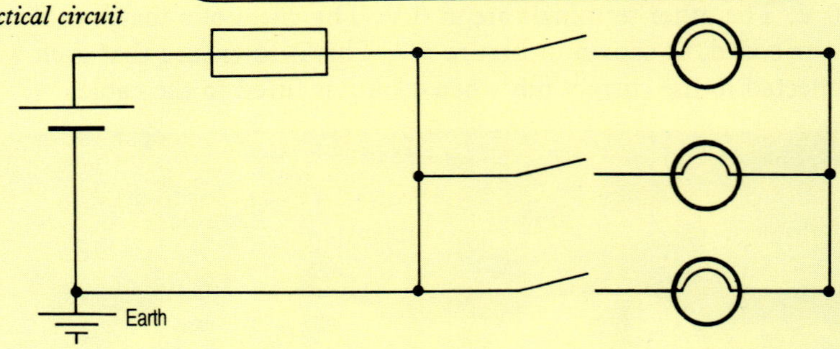

b *Circuit diagram*

Figure 5.11 A model lighting circuit

Paying for electricity

Every home has an electricity meter that registers the electrical energy used by the occupants. They pay the electricity supplier for the amount of electrical energy used.

An average household uses millions of joules of electrical energy each day. The joule is too small for measuring how much energy a household uses. Domestic electricity meters give readings in **kilowatt hours (kWh)**. This is the amount of electrical energy used by a 1 kW appliance in 1 hour.

SELEB

L. Jones
28 Homewood Rd
Otwood
M51 9YZ

For advice, contact
Smith Square
Mancaster
Tel: 012 65718
or at any SELEB shop

METER READINGS PRESENT	PREVIOUS	UNITS	PENCE PER UNIT	AMOUNT	VAT %
31534	30092	1442	5.79	83.49	ZERO
	STANDING CHARGE			7.30	
	TOTAL NOW DUE			90.79	

PERIOD ENDED 18.6.90

Figure 5.12 Checking your bill

Checking your electricity bills

A quarterly electricity bill tells you how much you have to pay for the electricity you have used over three months. A typical bill is shown in Figure 5.12. The bill shows the meter reading at the start of the period and again at the end. The difference between the readings is the number of **units** of electricity used. Each unit is 1 kWh of electrical energy.

The **unit cost** of electricity is the price of one unit (ie 1 kWh). The unit cost is multiplied by the number of units used to give the cost of the electricity used. A **standing charge** is then added on by the electricity supplier to cover the rental of the electricity meter.

Summary

An appliance connected to the mains is supplied with electricity through two wires – the live wire and the neutral wire. The ring-main circuit in a house includes a third wire, the earth wire. Electrical energy supplied to homes is measured in kilowatt hours.

Questions

1 A 240 V mains lighting circuit is used to supply ten 100 W, 240 V torch bulbs, each operated independently.

a Work out the current taken by each bulb.

b What is the total current supplied to the circuit when all the bulbs are on?

c How many kilowatt hours of electrical energy are used when all the lights are on for 6 h?

2 a A ring-main circuit has six wall sockets. Are these sockets in series or in parallel with each other?

b A 240 V, 100 W table lamp is connected to one socket and a 240 V, 2000 W heater to another. None of the other sockets are in use. How much current must be supplied to the ring main?

3 Karen recorded her electricity meter reading every seven days for three weeks. The readings were:

21731 21942 22150 22395

a Work out the total number of units used.

b On average, how many units were used each day?

c One week was much colder than the others. Which week do you think it was?

d Work out the average weekly cost of electricity at 5.5p per unit during this period.

4 To check the power rating of an electric heater, Colin has switched every electric appliance in the house off. He notes the meter reading at 56712.3 and then switches the heater on for exactly 2 h. After this time, he switches the heater off and notes the meter reading again. This time it reads 56717.4.

a How many kilowatt hours did the heater use in this time?

b Work out the power supplied to the heater in kW.

5 Figure 5.13 shows an outline of a house extension which is to have two light sockets, each operated by a different switch. The wiring will be connected to a light socket in an existing room. Copy the diagram and show on your diagram how you would join the new sockets and switches to the mains. Show clearly which wires are live and which are neutral.

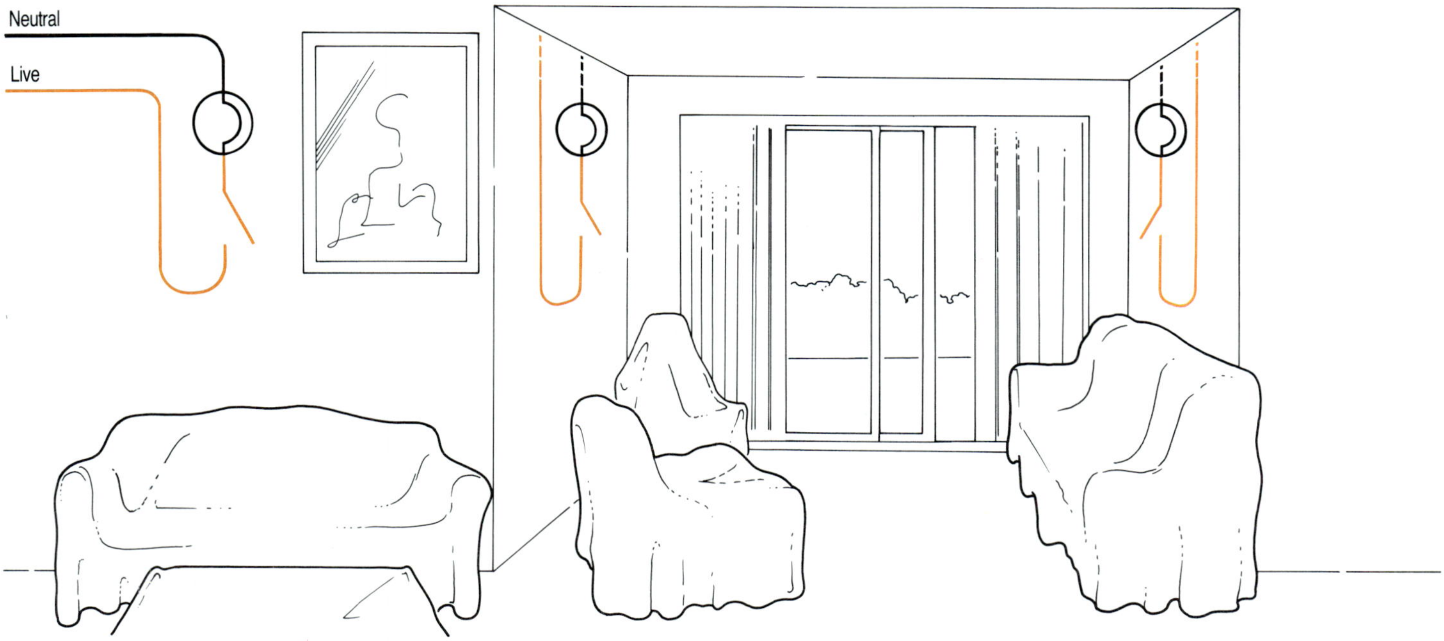

Figure 5.13

5.3 Safety matters

Mains electricity is extremely dangerous. The live wire of a mains circuit is at 240 V. Anyone touching a mains wire is likely to be electrocuted. Death is caused because the heart stops beating.

A current of as little as 100 mA can cause electrocution. Someone touching a live mains wire with one hand and the neutral wire with the other hand would almost certainly be electrocuted. The current would travel up one arm, through the chest and down the other arm. An electrician rewiring a house circuit will always turn the master switch OFF and remove the circuit fuse from the distribution box before starting rewiring.

The importance of earthing

The current a mains appliance takes passes into it via the live and neutral wires. The neutral wire is earthed at the local electricity substation. Fuses and switches are always on the live side of an appliance. They cut the appliance off from the live wire.

Ring-main circuits include an earth wire. This is used to connect the case or frame of an appliance to earth as near the distribution box as possible. If the case is not earthed and the live wire touches it, anyone touching the case will be electrocuted.

Figure 5.14 shows why an electric heater is made safer by earthing its frame. In **a**, the heater works normally and its frame is earthed. The frame can be touched safely. In **b**, the earth wire has broken. The frame would become live if the live wire touched it. In **c**, the heater element has touched the unearthed frame. Anyone touching the frame would be electrocuted. They would conduct electricity between the live frame and earth. In **d**, the earth wire has been repaired but the heater element still touches the frame. When the heater is switched on, current passes through part of the heater element via the live and earth wires. However, the frame is earthed so anyone touching it would not be electrocuted.

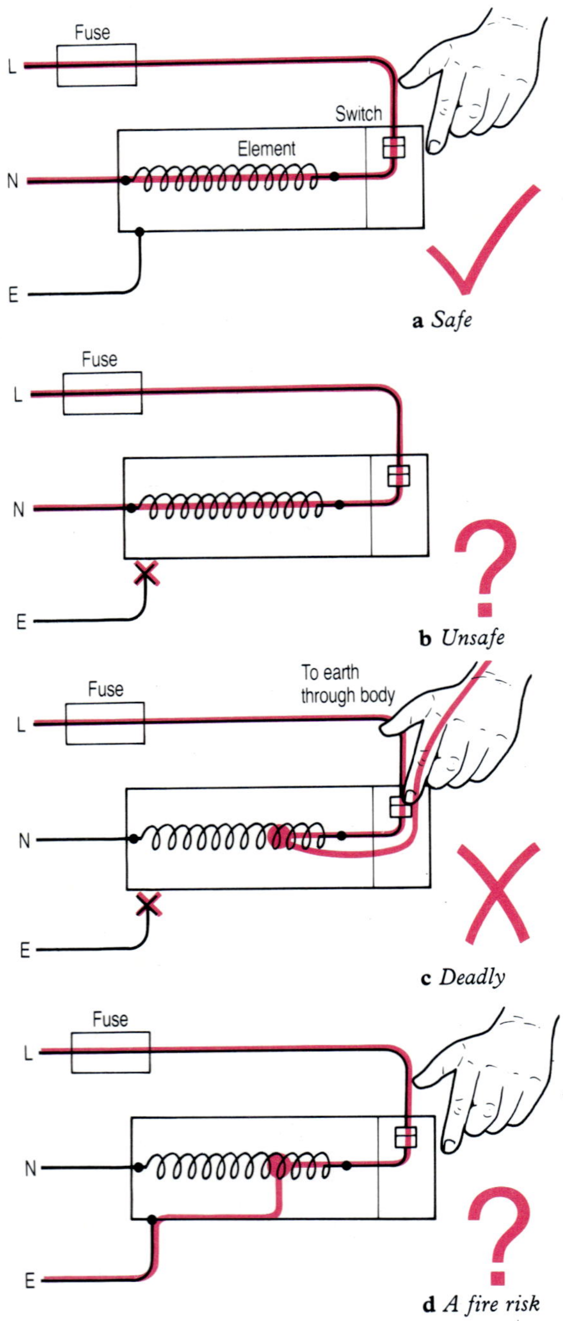

Figure 5.14 Earthing

Fuses

In Figure 5.14**d** the extra current passing along the live wire might not be enough to make the fuse blow. Suppose the normal current is 8.5 A and this increases to 11.5 A as a result of the fault. This would not be enough to blow a 13 A fuse. The fuse stops the current rising above a certain limit – it does not protect the user from electrocution.

If the fault causes the current to increase to more than 13 A, the fuse will blow and cut the current off. However, the fault might only increase the current a little.

The fuse in **c** provides no protection against electrocution either. Anyone touching the frame could be electrocuted by a current of as little as 100 mA. A small increase of current like this along the live wire would not be enough to blow the fuse. Fuses are designed to protect wiring and appliances from over heating if too much current passes through them.

> **Activity 5.3**
>
> **Why fuses blow**
>
> Graham's electric iron does not work. He thinks the fuse has blown. He takes the fuse to a local shop to buy a replacement. The shop assistant advises him to bring the iron in for repair.
>
> - Why should Graham take the iron in instead of buying a new fuse?

Circuit breakers

Mains appliances are designed to take current via the live and neutral wires. For an appliance operating normally, the same current passes along both the live wire and the neutral wire. Faults often cause the current in the two wires to differ. A **residual current circuit breaker (RCCB)** cuts the current off when this happens. The RCCB is said to 'trip' when it does this. An RCCB is shown in Figure 5.15.

RCCBs are designed to trip with currents of 30 mA or less. Figure 5.15**a** shows an electric heater connected to an RCCB. If the heating element touches the earthed frame, extra current passes along the live wire

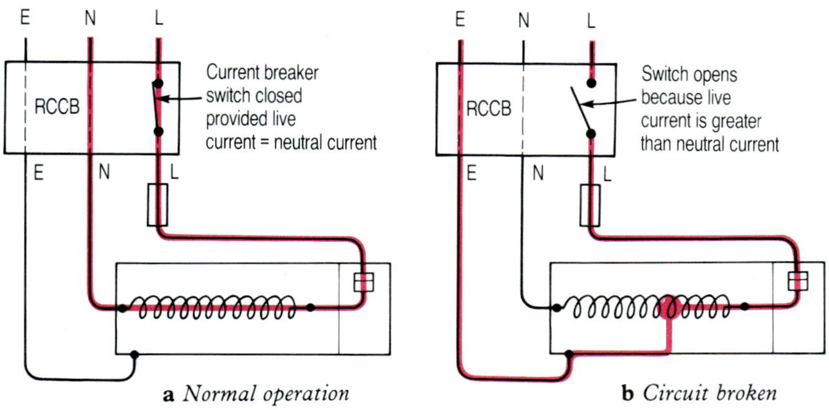

Figure 5.15 A circuit breaker

but not along the neutral wire. This trips the RCCB, as Figure 5.15**b** shows.

If the frame is not earthed and the heating element touches it, it becomes live. Anyone touching the frame trips the RCCB. This happens very quickly so the current is cut off before it becomes large enough to cause electrocution.

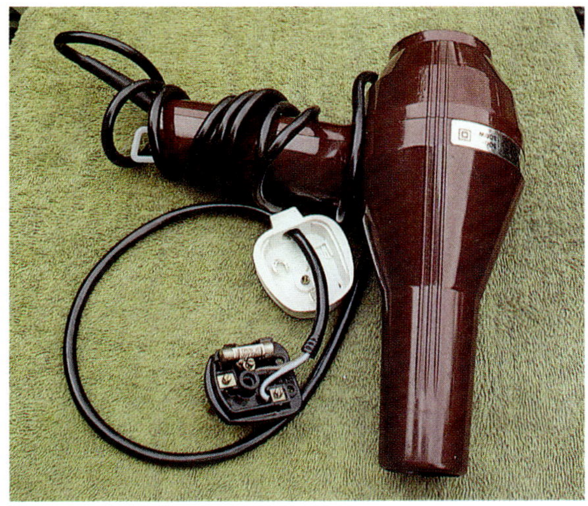

Figure 5.16 Look for the double insulation symbol

Double insulation

Kate's hair dryer does not have an earth wire. The flex consists of a live and a neutral wire only. The case of the hair dryer is plastic so cannot be earthed. The case has a double wall to provide an extra layer of electrical insulation. Figure 5.16 shows the symbol for double insulation.

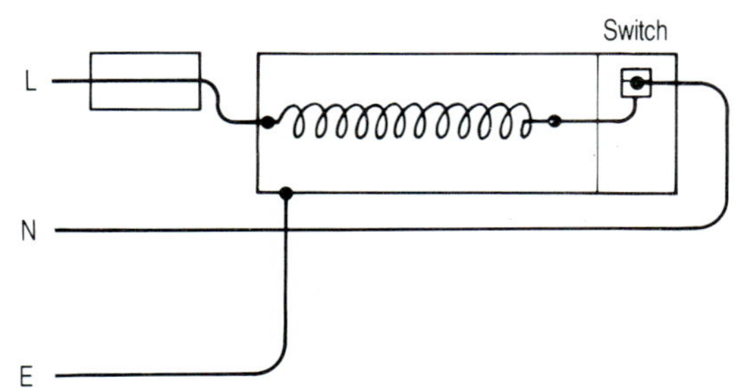

Figure 5.17

Summary

Earthing is used to prevent the frame or case of an appliance becoming live. Fuses prevent too much current passing through wiring and appliances.

Questions

1 Switches are always on the live side of appliances.
  a Would a switch work on the neutral side?
  b Why are switches always on the live side?

2 Figure 5.17 shows an electric heater which has been wired incorrectly.
  a Does the heater work when the switch is ON?
  b When the heater is OFF, why is it dangerous to touch the element?
  c What should be done to rewire the circuit correctly?

3 In circuit **c** of Figure 5.14, the unearthed frame has become live.
  a Why would it be dangerous to touch the frame?
  b The fuse does not provide any protection from electrocution. Why?

4 Design and make a model electric heater, operated at a low voltage, to explain the principle of earthing to your friends. Figure 5.18 shows some ideas to help you.

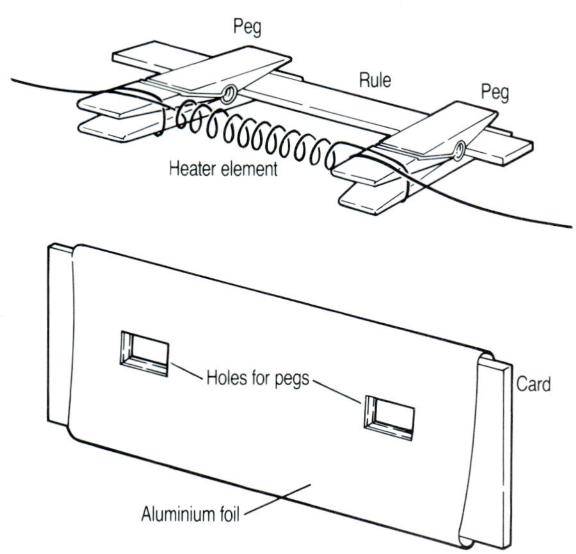

Figure 5.18

Unit 6
Resistance

6.1 Measuring resistance

Have you ever had to push your way through a crowd of people? Your motion is opposed or resisted by the crowd. Electrons passing through a torch bulb have to push their way through lots of atoms. The atoms **resist** the passage of electrons through the filament of the torch bulb.

Suppose a 3 V torch can be fitted with either a 0.25 A or a 0.35 A torch bulb. Which resists the flow of electrons most? The voltage is the same, so the torch bulb with the bigger resistance is the one that lets through the smaller current – ie the 0.25 A torch bulb.

The **resistance** of an electrical component is defined:

$$\text{Resistance} = \frac{\text{voltage}}{\text{current}}$$

$$R = \frac{V}{I}$$

Figure 6.1 shows how to use this equation.

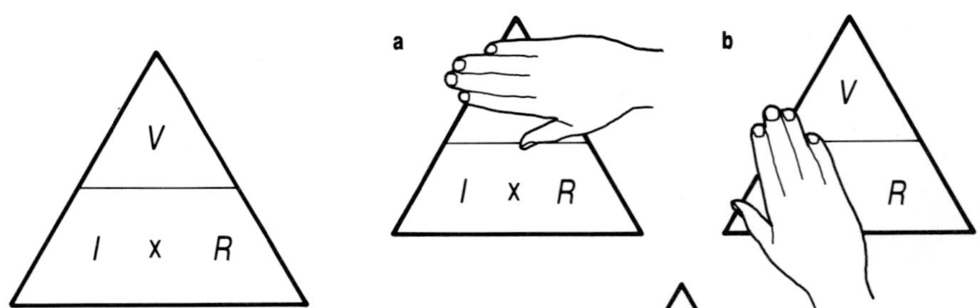

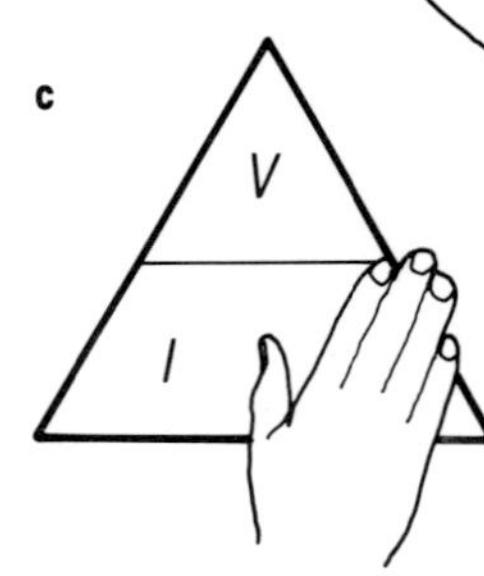

a *To work out V, use* $V = I \times R$

b *To work out I, use* $I = \frac{V}{R}$

c *To work out R, use* $R = \frac{V}{I}$

Figure 6.1 Using $R = \frac{V}{I}$

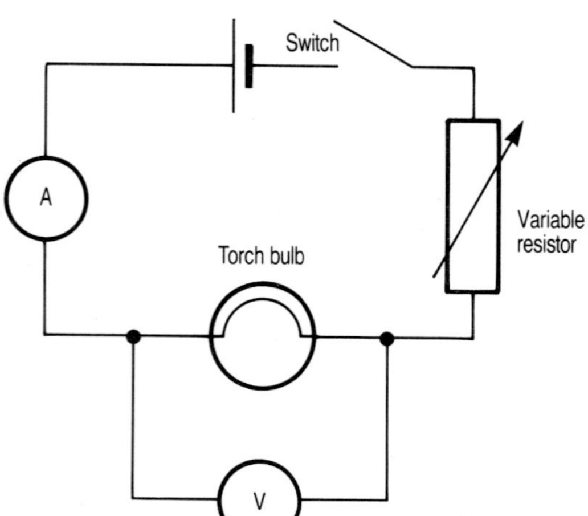

Figure 6.2 Investigating resistance

The unit of resistance is the **ohm**. The symbol for the ohm is the Greek letter Ω (omega).

- How does the resistance or a torch bulb vary with the voltage across it?
- How does the resistance of a torch bulb (which contains a filament of very thin wire) compare with that of a length of thick wire?

The circuit in Figure 6.2 may be used to find out.

The variable resistor is adjusted to vary the current in steps. At each step, the current and voltage are read from the meters. The process is repeated, replacing the bulb with a thick wire. Some typical measurements are given in Table 6.1.

The measurements may be plotted on a graph of voltage against current, as in Figures 6.3 and 6.4.

Torch bulb					
Current (A)	0.05	0.10	0.15	0.20	0.25
Voltage (V)	0.20	0.50	1.00	1.90	3.50
Wire					
Current (A)	0.05	0.10	0.15	0.20	0.25
Voltage (V)	0.50	1.00	1.50	2.00	2.50

Table 6.1

Figure 6.4 for thick wire shows that the voltage is proportional to the current. In other words, doubling the voltage makes the current double, etc. The resistance (voltage/current) is always the same for the wire. This was first discovered by Georg Ohm.

Figure 6.3 for the torch bulb shows that the graph curves towards the voltage axis. The voltage is *not* proportional to the current. To double the current, the voltage must be more than doubled. In other words, the resistance (voltage/ current) increases as the current increases. For example, at 0.1 A, the resistance of the torch bulb is 0.5 V/0.1 A = 5 Ω. However, at 0.2 A, the resistance is 1.9 V/0.2 A = 9.5 Ω.

The torch bulb resistance increases if the current is increased because the filament becomes hotter at a higher current. The atoms of the filament vibrate more when the filament is made hotter and so the flow of electrons is resisted more.

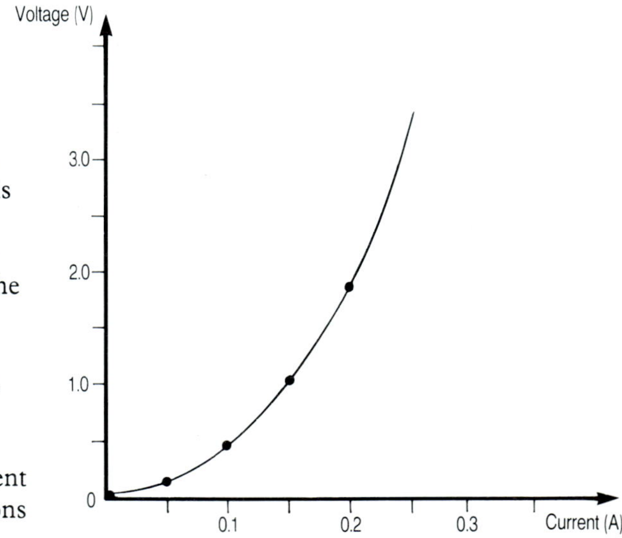

Figure 6.3 Voltage against current for a torch bulb

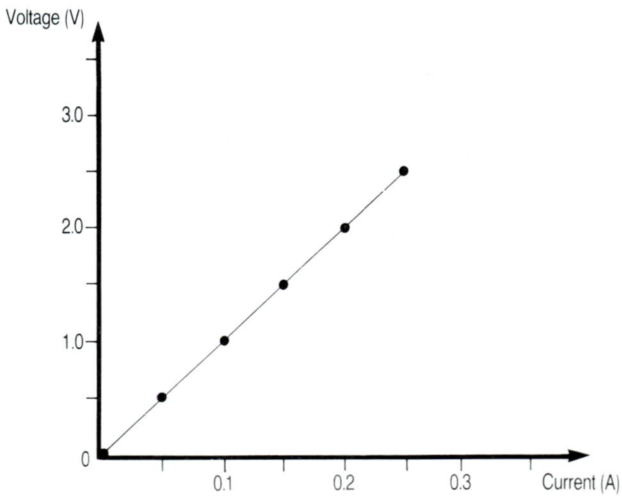

Figure 6.4 Voltage against current for a wire

Activity 6.1

Comparing torch bulbs

Two torch bulbs in turn are tested in the circuit of Figure 6.2. The measurements for each bulb are shown on the same graph in Figure 6.5.

1 Each bulb is rated at 3 V for normal operation. Use the graph to read off the current taken by each bulb at 3 V.

2 Work out the resistance of each bulb at 3 V.

3 The electrical power used by a device is given by current x voltage. How much power is used by each bulb in normal operation?

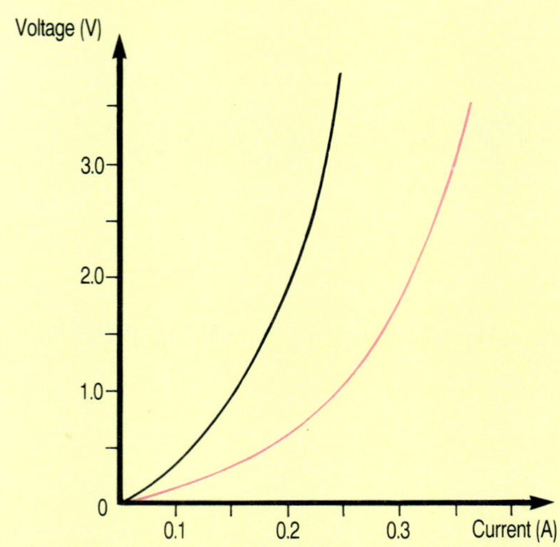

Figure 6.5

Figure 6.6 Georg Simon Ohm (1787–1854)

Georg Ohm

Georg Ohm (see Figure 6.6) developed the idea of electrical resistance which is the basis of electrical circuit theory. Ohm's Law states that the current through a wire under constant physical conditions is proportional to the voltage across it. In other words, the resistance of a wire at constant temperature is fixed and does not depend on the current passed through it.

Summary

Resistance is measured in ohms and is worked out from the equation resistance = voltage/current. The resistance of a metal increases if the temperature is increased.

Questions

1 Use the measurements in Table 6.1 to work out the resistance of the torch bulb at **a** 0.05 A **b** 0.15 A **c** 0.25 A.

2 Use the equation for resistance to work out

a the resistance of a wire that passes a current of 2 A when a voltage of 12 V is applied across it

b the voltage across a wire of resistance 4 Ω when it passes a current of 1.5 A

c the current through a 3 Ω wire with a voltage of 12 V across its ends.

3 A diode passes current in one direction only. The circuit of Figure 6.7 may be used to find out how the current passed by a diode varies with voltage. The variable resistor is used to vary the voltage. At each voltage, the voltmeter and ammeter readings are measured and recorded. Typical measurements are shown on the graph of current against voltage.

a What can you say about the diode's resistance in the forward direction compared with its resistance in the reverse direction?

b How does the 'forward' resistance change if the current is increased?

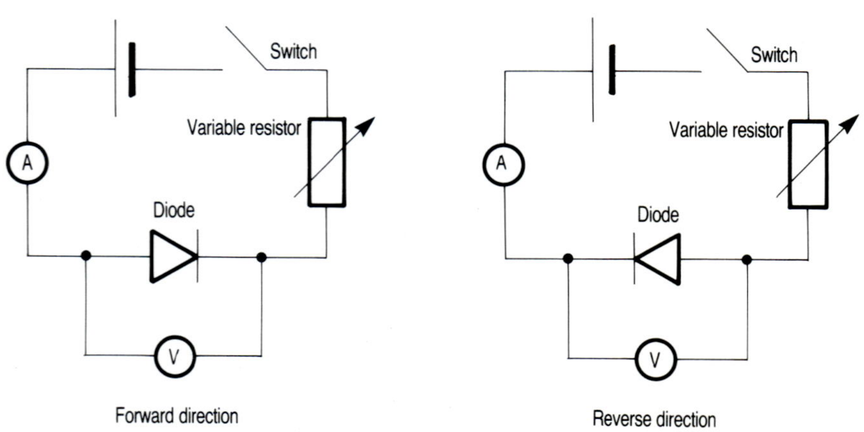

a *Testing a diode*

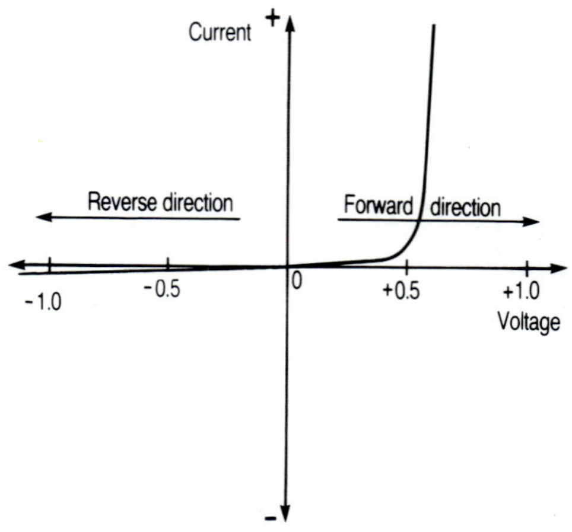

b *Typical results*

Figure 6.7

4 Karen and Helen want to use the circuit in Figure 6.8 to compare the resistance of two wires. They use the voltmeter to measure the voltage across each wire in turn. Their readings were:

3.5 V across wire P
2.5 V across wire Q

a Are the two wires in series or in parallel?
b What can you say about the current passing through each wire?
c Karen reckons that wire P has more resistance than wire Q. Helen does not think it is possible to say which wire has most resistance because the current has not been measured. Explain who you think is right.

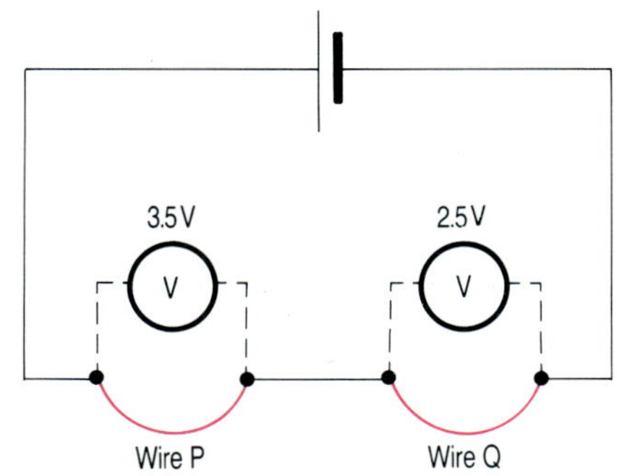

Figure 6.8

6.2 Make a resistor

A **resistor** is a component designed and made to have a known resistance. Some different types of resistors are shown in Figure 6.9. Resistors are used in circuits to limit the amount of current.

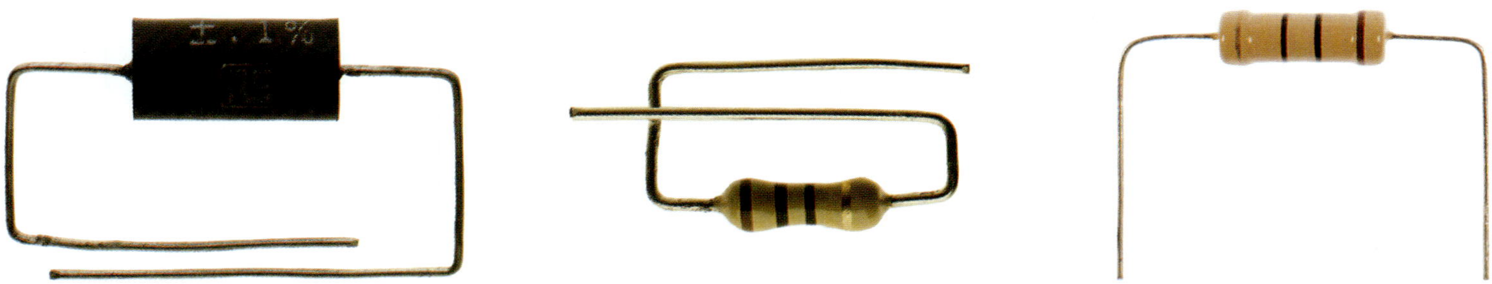
a *A wire-wound resistor* **b** *A carbon resistor* **c** *A high-resistance resistor*

Figure 6.9 Different types of resistors

For example, suppose a 2.5 V, 0.25 A motor is to be operated normally from a 3 V battery. If the motor is connected directly to the battery, it will run faster than normal because the 3 V battery will push more than 0.25 A through the motor. A resistor *in series* with the motor is needed to limit the current to 0.25 A. Figure 6.10 shows the circuit.

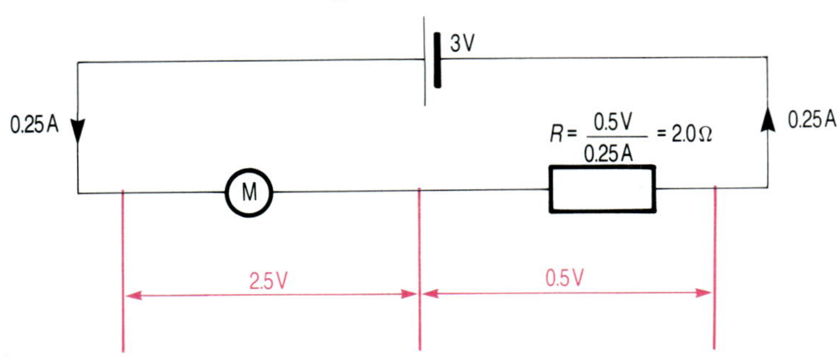

Figure 6.10 Working out resistance

● What should the resistance of the resistor be?

The battery voltage (3 V) is shared between the motor (2.5 V) and the resistor. The resistor voltage must therefore be 0.5 V. The current through the resistor is the same as that through the motor, which is 0.25 A. The resistance of the resistor is therefore:

$$R = \frac{V}{I} = \frac{0.5\text{ V}}{0.25\text{ A}} = 2\ \Omega$$

Activity 6.2

How to make a 2 Ω resistance

1. Use the circuit of Figure 6.11 to find out how the resistance of a wire varies with the length of the wire. Test different measured lengths of the same wire.
2. For each length, measure and record the current and voltage.
3. Use the equation for resistance to work out the resistance, in ohms, of each length of wire.
4. Use your results to plot a graph of resistance (on the vertical axis) against length.
   Figure 6.12 shows a typical graph. The resistance is proportional to the length.
5. Read off the length from your graph that is needed to make a 2 Ω resistor.

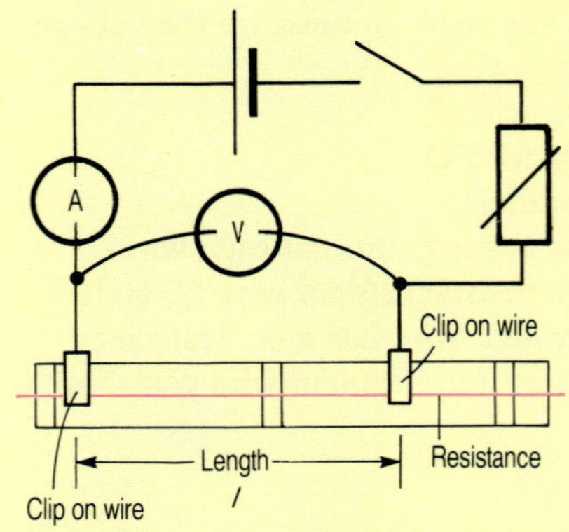

Figure 6.11 Measuring the resistance of a wire

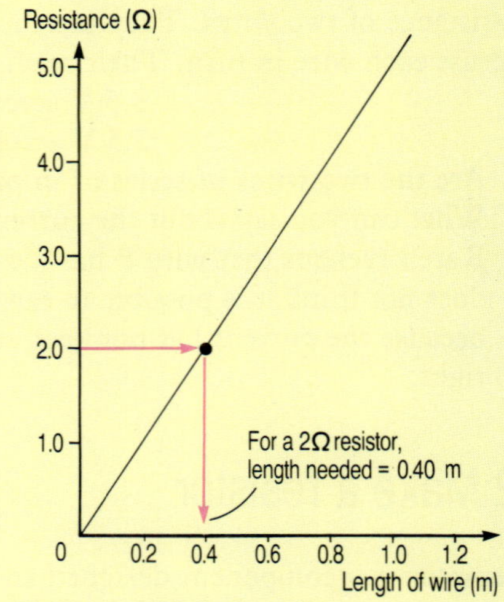

Figure 6.12 Typical results

Activity 6.3

A reel problem

Simon has found an unlabelled reel of wire which he thinks is made from a alloy called constantan. He wants to measure its resistance and then use a data book to see if the resistance is correct for constantan.

1. Sketch a circuit diagram to measure the resistance of the wire.
2. He measures the resistance of 10 m of wire. It gives the result 7.2 Ω. The data books gives the measurements in Table 6.2 for different diameters of constantan.

Diameter (mm)	0.914	0.711	0.559	0.457	0.376
Resistance per metre (Ω)	0.72	1.20	1.93	2.89	4.27

Table 6.2

- Do you think the wire tested could be made from constantan?
- What additional test could you do to confirm this?

Summary

The resistance of a wire is proportional to its length.

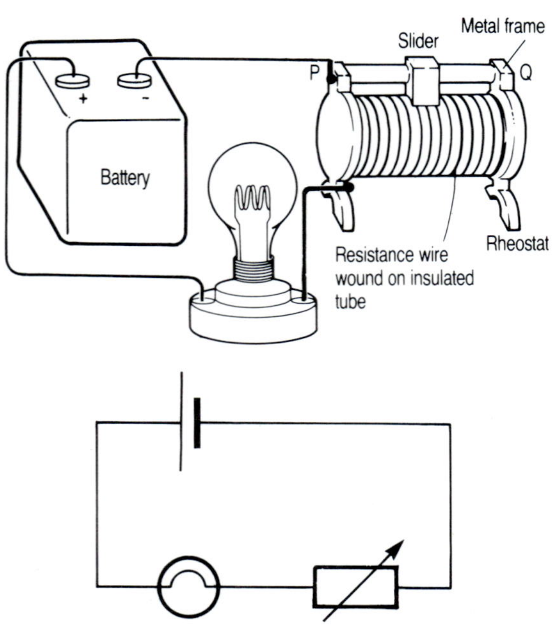

Figure 6.13

Questions

1. In Figure 6.12 what is the resistance of
   a 0.5 m of wire **b** 1 m of wire **c** 10 m of wire?
2. A length of 10 m of a certain wire has a resistance of 6.5 Ω. Work out
   a the resistance per metre of the wire
   b the length needed to make a resistance of 2 Ω.
3. Figure 6.13 shows a variable resistor (or rheostat) in a circuit to control the brightness of a lamp.
   a Explain why the current through the lamp changes when the slider is moved.
   b The slider is moved towards end P of the rheostat. Does this make the lamp brighter or dimmer? Explain.
4. Given different thicknesses of wire of the same material, design an experiment to find out how the resistance of a wire depends on its diameter.

6.3 Sensors

Automatic street lights switch on at dusk and switch off at dawn. Each street light has a **sensor** which detects the natural light intensity. Different sensors are available that can detect other changes, such as temperature or pressure changes.

Activity 6.4

Sensor resistors

1 Connect a **light-dependent resistor** (LDR) in series with a milliammeter and a battery, as shown in Figure 6.14.
- What happens to the meter reading when the LDR is covered, then uncovered?
- What does this tell you about the LDR's resistance?

2 Replace the LDR with a **thermistor.**
- What difference is made to the meter reading when the thermistor is warmed?
- What does this tell you about the resistance of the thermistor?

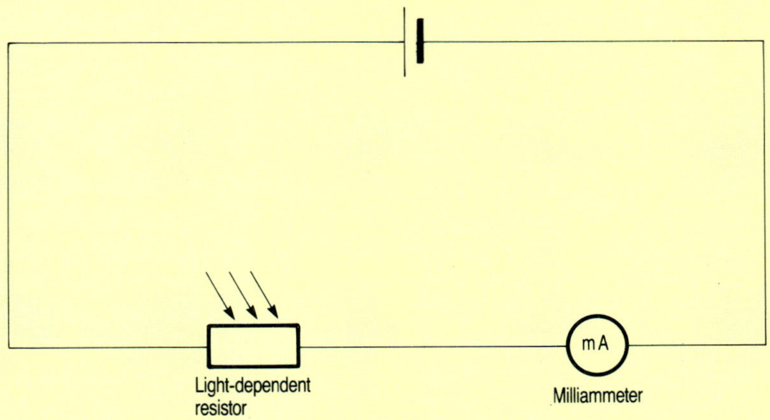

Figure 6.14 Testing an LDR

Activity 6.5

The potential divider

A **potential divider** consists of two or more resistors in series joined to a battery. The battery voltage is shared between the resistors.

Try the following tests using the circuit in Figure 6.15. Copy Table 6.3 and use your results to complete it.

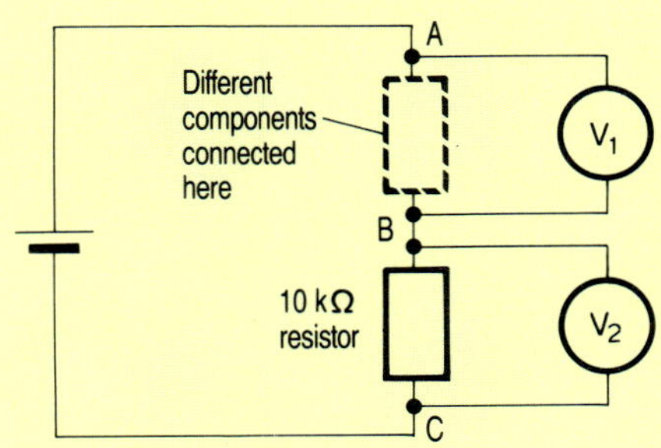

Figure 6.15 A potential divider

Resistor in gap AB	Action	Voltmeter readings
1 10 kΩ	None	V_1 = 0.75 V V_2 = 0.75 V
2 20 kΩ	None	V_1 = 1 V V_2 = 0.5 V
3 Variable resistor	Increase variable resistance	
4 LDR	Cover then uncover LDR	
5 Thermistor	Warm thermistor	

Table 6.3

- Can you explain these results?

1 There are two equal resistors so the battery voltage is shared equally between them.
2 There is more resistance in the gap so a bigger share of the battery voltage is taken up across the gap. As a result there is less voltage across the other resistor.
3, 4 and **5** Think about the change of resistance in the gap causing a different share of the battery voltage across the gap.

Make a light sensor

The potential divider in Figure 6.16 is used to supply the input voltage to a NOT gate. A low-power buzzer is connected between the output terminal of the NOT gate and the 0 V line.

- What happens when the LDR is covered, and then uncovered?

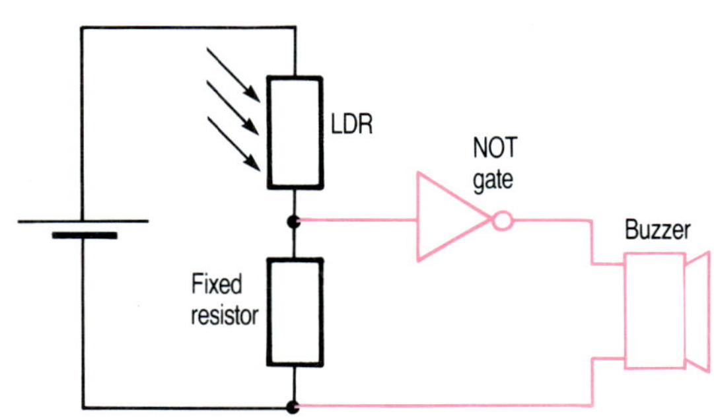

Figure 6.16 A light sensor

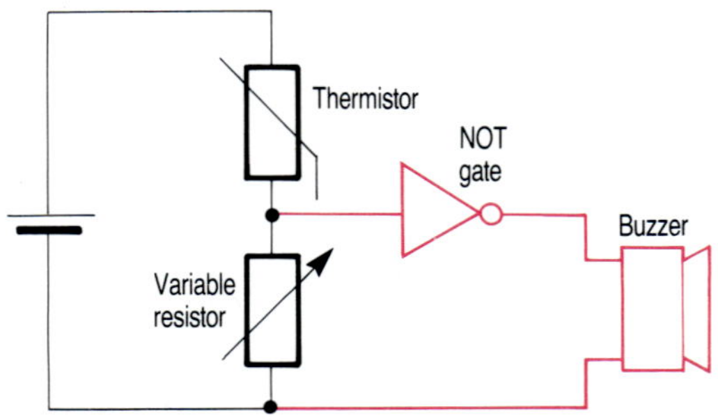

Figure 6.17 A low-temperature alarm

The buzzer sounds when the output state of the NOT gate is high (ie 1). To make this happen, the input state of the NOT gate must be low (ie 0).

Covering the LDR increases its resistance and this reduces the share of the battery voltage across the fixed resistor. The input voltage falls and the buzzer sounds. The system is a simple light sensor.

Suppose the fixed resistor is replaced by a variable resistor. The buzzer can now be made to sound at different light levels by adjusting the variable resistor.

If the LDR is replaced with a thermistor, the circuit operates as a low-temperature buzzer. Figure 6.17 shows the circuit. Cooling the thermistor by placing it in icy water makes the buzzer sound.

Sensors and microcomputers

Microcomputers can be used to take and display readings and to control experiments. Sensors are connected to microcomputers through special circuits called **interfaces**. These circuits convert the voltage from a sensor into signals which the microcomputer can read. They also protect the microcomputer's own circuits.

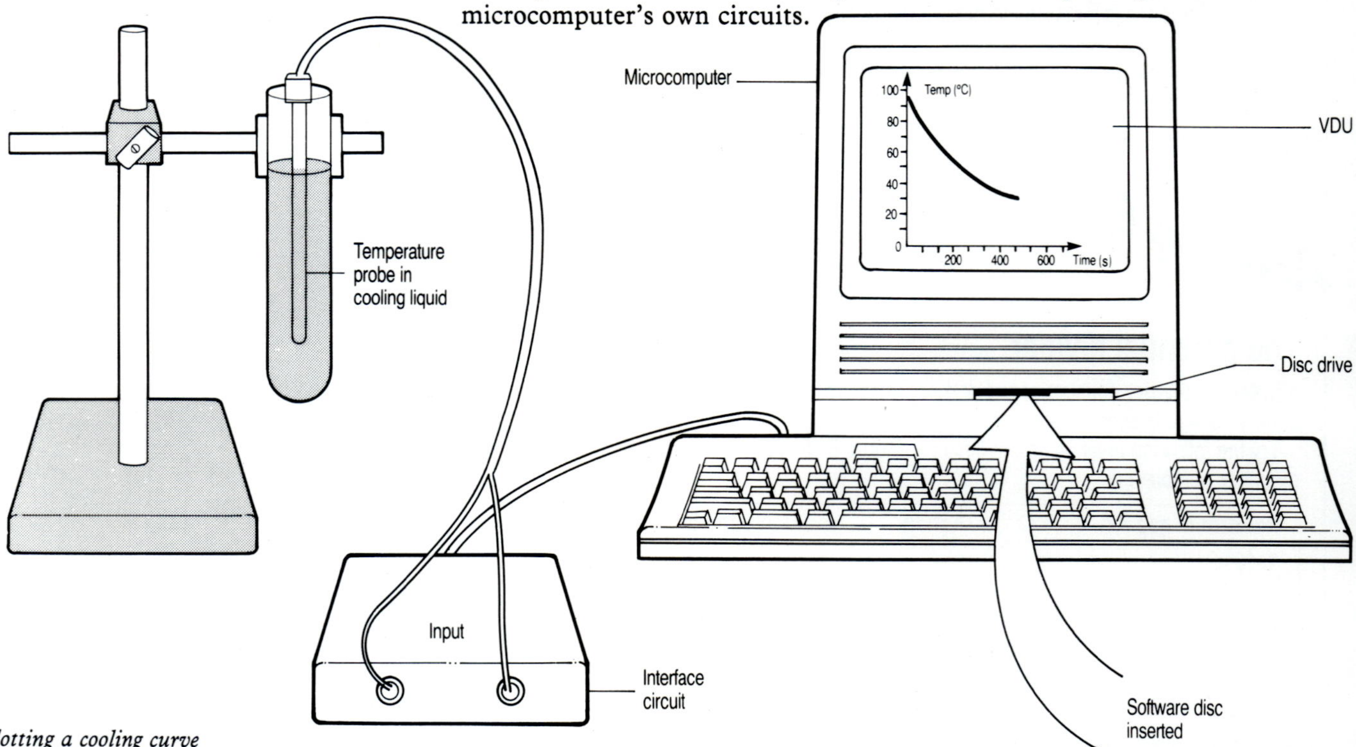

Figure 6.18 Plotting a cooling curve

Figure 6.18 shows a microcomputer used to monitor temperature. The microcomputer is programmed to read the voltage from the sensor and to work out and display the temperature.

With different sensors and programs, a microcomputer can be used as a scientific instrument with a wide range of applications.

Summary

In a potential divider, the battery voltage is shared between the resistors. The voltage across each resistor is in proportion to its resistance.

Questions

1 An LDR is covered, and then uncovered.
  a How does its resistance alter?
  b If the LDR is part of a circuit, how does the current through it alter when it is covered and then uncovered?

2 Two 100 Ω resistors are joined in series and connected to a 6 V battery.
  a Sketch the circuit.
  b What is the voltage across each resistor?
  c What is the current through each resistor?

3 A variable resistor and a 100 Ω resistor are used to make a potential divider to be connected to a 6 V battery. The 100 Ω resistor is connected to the positive terminal of the battery.
  a Sketch the circuit.
  b The variable resistor is adjusted until the battery voltage is shared equally between the two resistors. What is the resistance of the variable resistor set at?
  c The resistance of the variable resistor is then increased to 200 Ω. What is the voltage across the fixed resistor now?

4 A thermistor and a variable resistor form a potential divider, as shown in Figure 6.19.

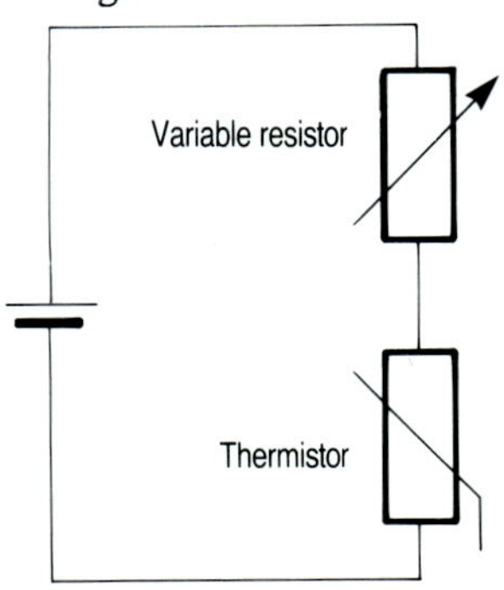

Figure 6.19

  a What happens to the voltage across the variable resistor when the thermistor is warmed?
  b How could you use this with a suitable logic gate and buzzer as a high-temperature alarm?

5 Figure 6.18 shows a temperature sensor connected to a microcomputer. The system is used to investigate temperature changes when different salts are dissolved in water. When the program is run, the probe temperature is measured every second for five minutes. The measurements are shown on the VDU as a graph of temperature against time.
  a How could you check that the system is reliable?
  b Design an investigation to find out how the mass of salt dissolved affects the temperature change.

6.4 Resistor combination rules

Activity 6.6

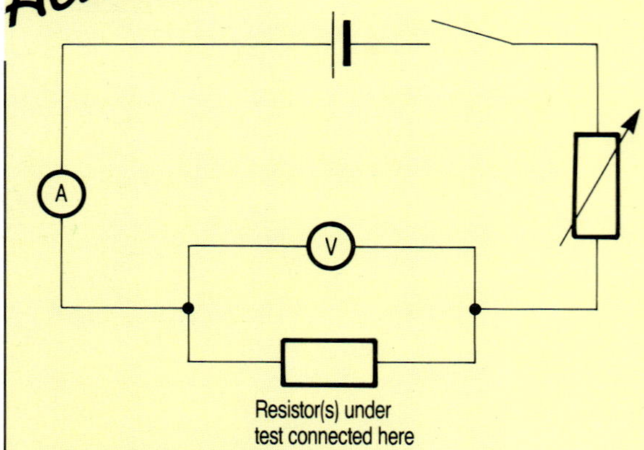

Figure 6.20 Testing resistors

Resistors in series

Ayesha and Kate used the circuit in Figure 6.20 to investigate resistor combinations. They measured the resistance of some resistors. Then they connected different pairs of resistors in series and measured the resistance of each pair. Their results are shown in Table 6.4.

Resistance of individual resistors	Resistance of series combinations
1 A = 2.0 Ω B = 4.0 Ω	A and B in series = 6.0 Ω
2 A = 2.0 Ω C = 2.5 Ω	A and C in series = 4.5 Ω
3 B = 4.0 Ω C = 2.5 Ω	B and C in series = 6.5 Ω

Table 6.4

Ayesha and Kate concluded that the combined resistance is equal to the sum of the individual resistances. Test this using your own circuit and resistors.

Combined resistances in series

Two resistors R_1 and R_2 are in series, as shown in Figure 6.21. The same current passes through both resistors because they are in series.

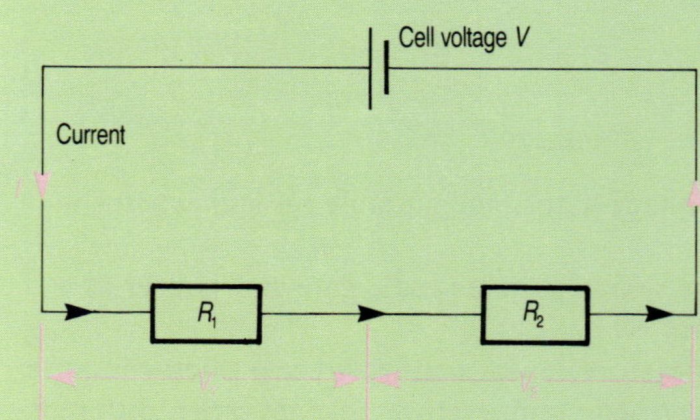

Figure 6.21 Resistors in series

Using the equation:

$$\text{Resistance} = \frac{\text{voltage}}{\text{current}}$$

the voltage across each resistor can be worked out from multiplying the current and the resistance.

Voltage across $R_1 = I \times R_1$

Voltage across $R_2 = I \times R_2$ where I is the current

Since the total voltage V across R_1 and R_2 is shared between R_1 and R_2, then:

$$V = V_1 + V_2$$

giving $$V = IR_1 + IR_2 = I(R_1 + R_2)$$

The combined resistance $R = \dfrac{\text{total voltage } V}{\text{current } I}$

$$R = \frac{I(R_1 + R_2)}{I}$$

$$R = R_1 + R_2$$

The theory shows that the combined resistance R is equal to the sum of the individual resistances.

Combined resistances in parallel

Two resistors R_1 and R_2 are connected in parallel to a battery of voltage V, as shown in Figure 6.22.

- How much current passes through each resistor?

The voltage across each resistor is V (because they are in parallel). For each resistor:

$$\text{Current} = \frac{\text{voltage}}{\text{resistance}}$$

therefore the current I_1 through resistor R_1 is given by:

$$I_1 = \frac{V}{R_1}$$

and current I_2 through the resistor R_2 by:

$$I_2 = \frac{V}{R_2}$$

The battery current is:

$$I = I_1 + I_2 = \frac{V}{R_1} + \frac{V}{R_2}$$

Since the combined resistance is:

$$R = \frac{\text{battery voltage}}{\text{battery current } I}$$

then $$I = \frac{V}{R}$$

giving $$\frac{V}{R} = \frac{V}{R_1} + \frac{V}{R_2}$$

Cancelling V from both sides therefore gives the rule for two resistors in parallel:

$$\frac{1}{R} = \frac{1}{R_1} + \frac{1}{R_2}$$

Rearranging this equation to make R the subject gives:

$$\frac{1}{R} = \frac{R_2 + R_1}{R_1 \times R_2}$$

so $$R = \frac{R_1 \times R_2}{R_1 + R_2}$$

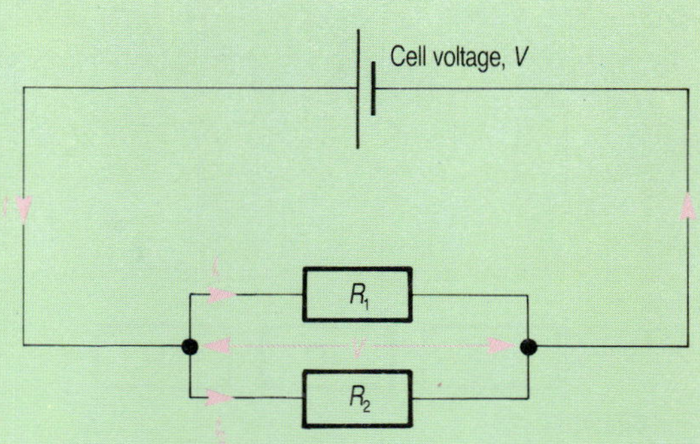

Figure 6.22 Resistors in parallel

Activity 6.7

Resistors in parallel

Table 6.5 shows some results from testing pairs of resistors in parallel.

- Work out the combined resistance from the individual resistances. Use the equation opposite.

Resistance of individual resistors
1 A = 2.0 Ω B = 4.0 Ω
2 A = 2.0 Ω C = 2.5 Ω
3 B = 4.0 Ω C = 2.5 Ω
4 B = 4.0 Ω D = 12.0 Ω
Resistance of parallel combinations
A and B in parallel = 1.3 Ω
A and C in parallel = 1.1 Ω
B and C in parallel = 1.5 Ω
B and D in parallel = 3.0 Ω

Table 6.5

Do your calculations agree with the measured resistance of each combination?

Worked example

What is the combined resistance of a 5 Ω resistor and an 8 Ω resistor connected **a** in series **b** in parallel? (See Figure 6.23.)

Solution

a In series, the combined resistance is 8 Ω + 5 Ω = 13 Ω (the sum of the individual resistances).

b In parallel, the combined resistance R is given by:

$$\frac{1}{R} = \frac{1}{8} + \frac{1}{5} = 0.125 + 0.2 = 0.325$$

Hence: $$R = \frac{1}{0.325} = 3.1\ \Omega$$

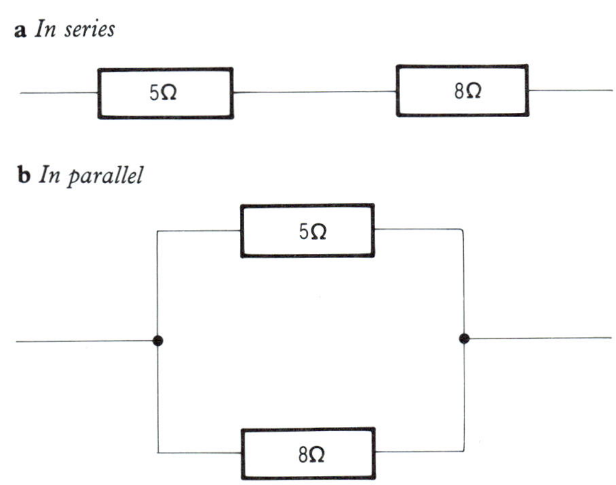

Figure 6.23

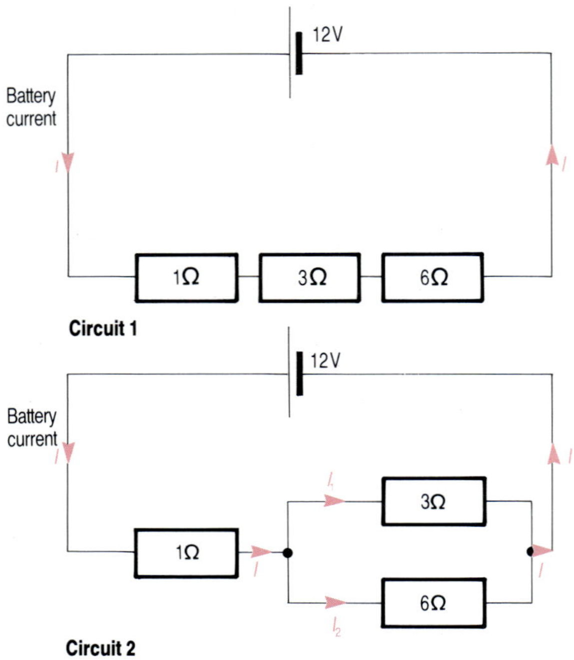

Figure 6.24 Circuit problems

Using the resistor combination rules

You need to know the rules to work out currents and voltages in circuits containing more than one resistor. Look at the circuits shown in Figure 6.24.

1 In Circuit 1 the combined resistance of three resistors in series is the sum of the individual resistances, which equals 10 Ω here. This is the total resistance of the circuit.

$$\text{Battery current} = \frac{\text{battery voltage}}{\text{total resistance}} = \frac{12\ \text{V}}{10\ \Omega} = 1.2\ \text{A}$$

Voltage across each resistor = current × resistance

hence Voltage across 1 Ω resistor = 1.2 A × 1 Ω = 1.2 V

Voltage across 3 Ω resistor = 1.2 A × 3 Ω = 3.6 V

Voltage across 6 Ω resistor = 1.2 A × 6 Ω = 7.2 V

Note that the battery voltage equals the sum of the resistor voltages (because the resistors are in series).

2 In circuit 2:

Step 1 To work out the total resistance, you need to first work out the combined resistance R of the 3 Ω resistor and the 6 Ω resistor in parallel. You can do this from the parallel combination rule.

$$\frac{1}{R} = \frac{1}{3} + \frac{1}{6} = 0.33 + 0.17 = 0.5$$

Hence: $R = 2\ \Omega$

This combined resistance is in series with the 1 Ω resistor. Hence the total resistance of the circuit is 3 Ω (2 Ω + 1 Ω).

Step 2 To work out the battery current:

$$\text{Battery current} = \frac{\text{battery voltage}}{\text{total resistance}} = \frac{12\ \text{V}}{3\ \Omega} = 4\ \text{A}$$

Step 3 How much current passes through each resistor?

a The 1 Ω resistor is in series with the battery. Hence the current passing through it is 4 A (the same as the battery current).

b The current through the 1 Ω resistor splits between the 3 Ω and the 6 Ω resistors. Let I_1 be the current through the 3 Ω resistor and I_2 the current through the 6 Ω resistor.

Hence: $I_1 + I_2 = 4$ A

Also, since Voltage = current × resistance,

Voltage across the 3 Ω resistor = $3 \times I_1$

and Voltage across the 6 Ω resistor = $6 \times I_2$

Since these two resistors are in parallel with each other, their voltages are equal:

$$3\,I_1 = 6\,I_2 \quad \text{so} \quad I_1 = 2\,I_2$$

Therefore $\boldsymbol{I_1}$ **= 2.67 A** and $\boldsymbol{I_2}$ **= 1.33 A** since $I_1 + I_2 = 4$

Summary

For two resistors R_1 and R_2 in series, the combined resistance R is $R_1 + R_2$. In parallel, the combined resistance R is given by

$$\frac{1}{R} = \frac{1}{R_1} + \frac{1}{R_2}.$$

Questions

1 Work out the combined resistance for each of the following pairs of resistors in series and in parallel

a 3 Ω and 6 Ω **b** 6 Ω and 12 Ω **c** 4 Ω and 4 Ω **d** 1 Ω and 2 Ω.

2 a Work out the total resistance of the resistor combinations in Figure 6.25.

b The rule for more than two resistors in parallel is:

$$\frac{1}{R} = \frac{1}{R_1} + \frac{1}{R_2} + \frac{1}{R_3} + \ldots$$

Work out the total resistance of a 3 Ω, a 6 Ω and a 12 Ω resistor in parallel.

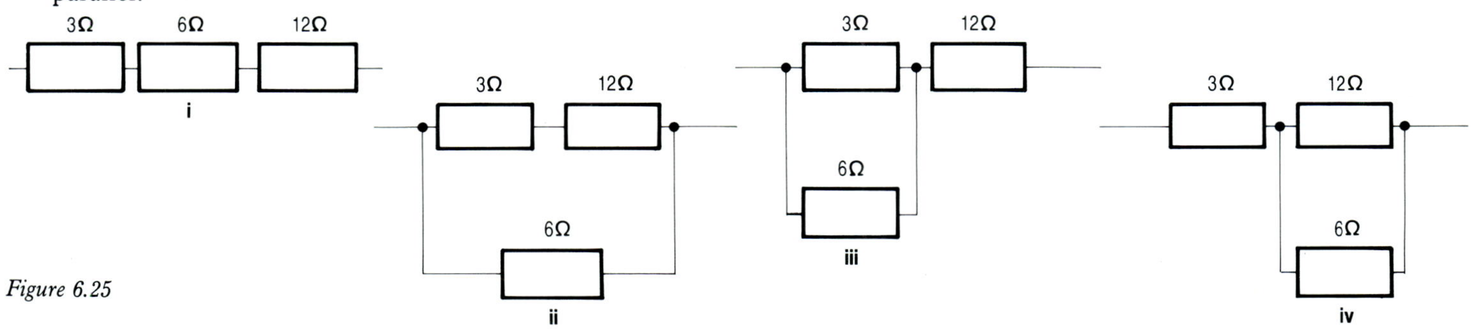

Figure 6.25

3 a A 6 Ω resistor is connected across a 6 V battery. Work out the current through the resistor.

b A 12 Ω resistor is connected in parallel with the 6 Ω resistor across the 6 V battery. Sketch the circuit and work out the current through each resistor and the battery current.

4 For each of the circuits shown in Figure 6.26, work out

a the total resistance of each circuit **b** the battery current in each circuit

c the current and voltage for each resistor in each circuit.

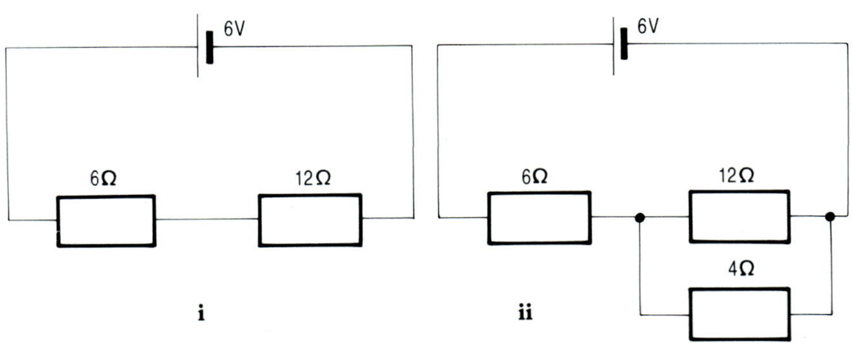

Figure 6.26

5 Two 4 Ω resistors and a 3 V battery are connected in series.

a Sketch the circuit and work out the current and voltage for each resistor.

b A third 4 Ω resistor is connected in parallel with one of the other resistors. Sketch the new circuit and work out the current and voltage for each resistor.

6.5 Resistance heating

Resistors become warm when current passes through them. The work done by electrons as they push through the atoms of a resistor heats the resistor. Figure 6.27 shows a setup to investigate the heating effect of a wire-wound resistor.

- How does the heat produced depend on the current?

Current (A)	0.0	0.5	1.0	1.5	2.0	2.5
Temperature rise (°C) in 300 s	0.0	0.5	2.0	5.0	8.0	13.0

Table 6.6

In Figure 6.27, different currents are used to heat the same volume of water for the same time. The temperature rise is measured. Typical results are shown in Table 6.6.

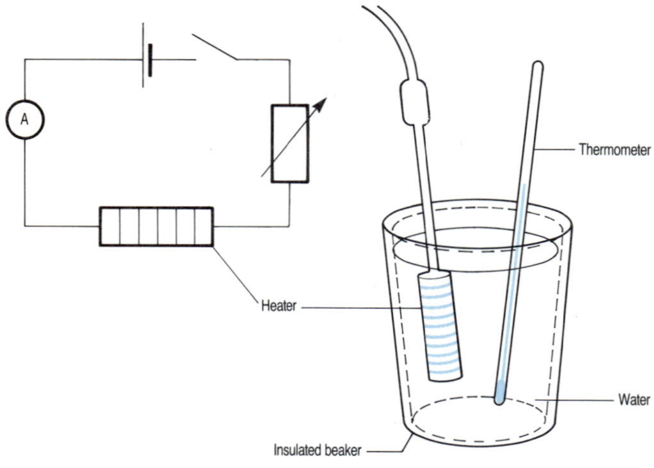

Figure 6.27 Electrical heating

The temperature rise is multiplied by 4 when the current is doubled. This suggests that the temperature rise is proportional to the square of the current.

- What graph would you plot to check this?

Power and heating

A current I passes through a resistor R. The voltage across the resistor is $I \times R$.

Power supplied to resistor $= I \times V$ (see page 32)
$= I^2 \times R$ (since $V = IR$)

In time t, electrical energy delivered = power × time = I^2Rt

The resistor converts the electrical energy supplied into heat.

Therefore **Heat produced =** $\boldsymbol{I^2 R t}$

Activity 6.8

Heater design

Hasan and Graham are designing a heater to be run off a 12 V battery. They want to use a coiled wire as the heating element.

They need to know whether a short length of wire produces more heat than a long length. Hasan thinks a short length will produce less heat. Graham thinks the current passing through a short length will be larger and so more heat will be produced.

- Who do you think is right?
- Devise a test to find out.

Practical heaters

The wire which produces heat in a heater is called the **heating element.** Figure 6.28 shows various types of heating elements. Each element is designed to work at a certain voltage. At this voltage, the heat produced per second is equal to its power rating.

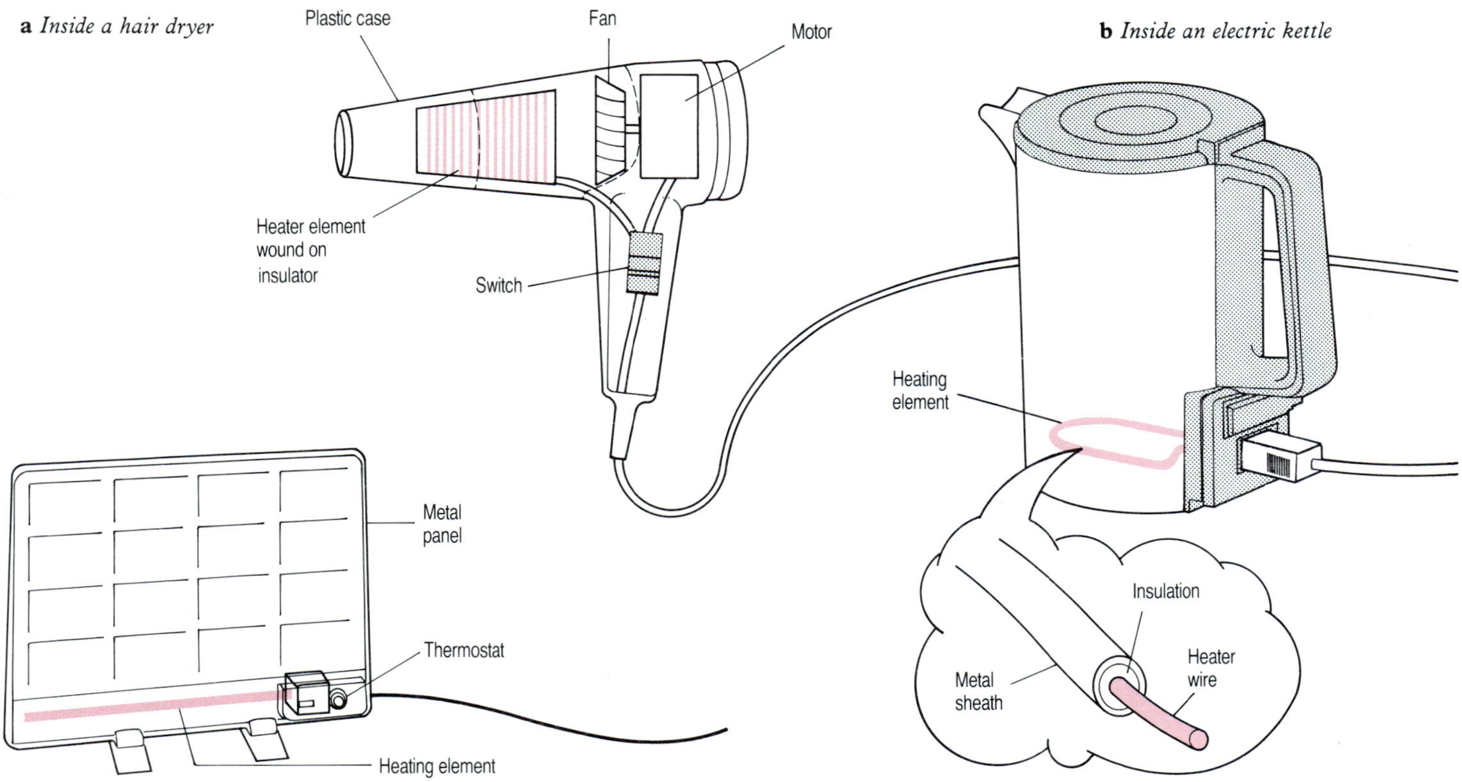

a *Inside a hair dryer*

b *Inside an electric kettle*

c *Inside an oil-filled radiator*

Figure 6.28 Heating elements

Summary

The heat produced by a resistor is proportional to the current squared.

Questions

1 A 6 Ω resistor is connected across the terminals of a 12 V battery. Work out **a** the current through the resistor **b** the heat produced by the resistor in 60 s.

2 **a** Use the results in Table 6.6 to plot a graph of temperature rise (on the vertical axis) against the square of the current.

b What would be the temperature rise for
i a current of 3 A for 300 s **ii** a current of 2 A for 600 s?

3 A 10 Ω resistor is stamped with the label '10 Ω, 1 W'. This means it should not use more than 1 W of power.

a How much power would it use if it was connected to a 3 V battery?

b Why should it not be used at voltages higher than 3 V?

4 Part of the heating element of a hair dryer has formed a short-circuit. No current passes through this part but the rest of the element becomes dangerously hot. Why?

Unit 7
Electromagnetism

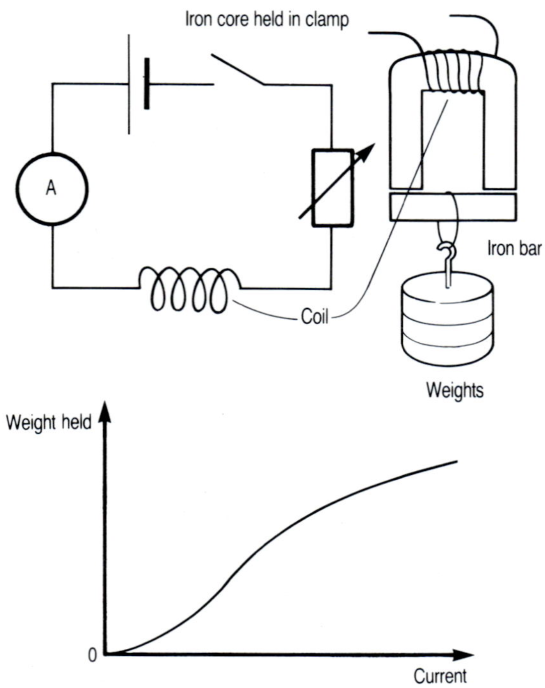

Figure 7.1 Testing an electromagnet

7.1 Electromagnets

● How much weight can an electromagnet hold?

Figure 7.1 shows how this can be investigated. The electromagnet's iron core is magnetised by the current passing through the coil. The weight the electromagnet can support increases as the current increases. However, the *increase* in weight gets less for equal increases in the current. Eventually, no *more* weight can be supported no matter how large the current. The strength of the electromagnet reaches an upper limit. After this no matter how much current passes through the coil, the strength does not increase. At this point the electromagnet is fully magnetised.

Switch off an electromagnet and you will find it does not lose its magnetism completely. The core retains some magnetism even though there is no current in the coil. Steel retains magnetism better than iron. That is why iron is used for the core of an electromagnet rather than steel.

Electromagnets in action

Figure 7.2 shows two devices that use electromagnets. The electromagnet attracts a piece of iron when both devices are switched on.

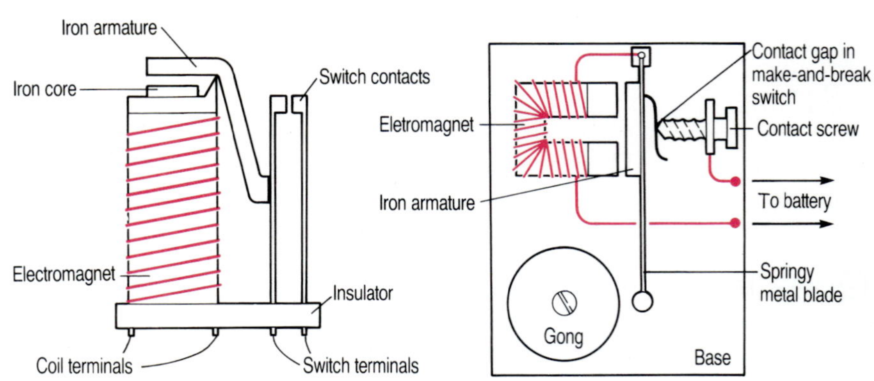

a *The relay* **b** *The electric bell*

Figure 7.2 Using electromagnets

Activity 7.1

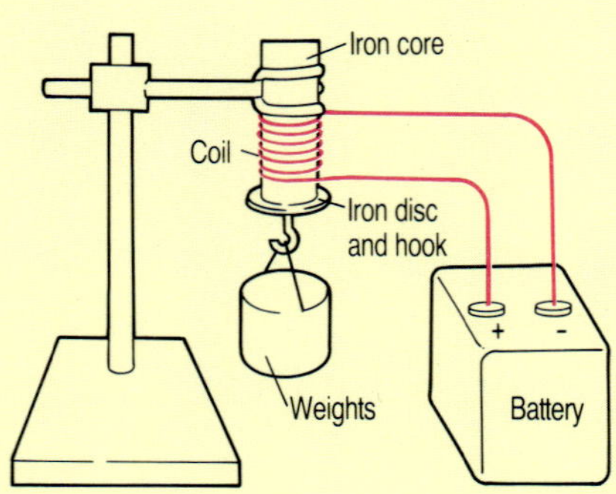

Figure 7.3

Number of turns	0	4	5	6	7	8	9	10
Weight held (newtons)	0.0	0.0	0.3	1.0	1.5	2.0	3.5	4.5

Table 7.1

The number of turns in a coil

Simon and Debbie are making an electromagnet using some insulated wire, an iron bar and a battery. Simon thinks as many turns as possible should be wound on the bar. Debbie reckons that too much wire will reduce the current and make the electromagnet weaker.

1 Design an experiment to find out how the weight held depends on the number of turns. Figure 7.3 shows one experiment that could be used. Table 7.1 shows some results from an experiment like this.
2 Plot a graph of weight held against number of turns.
3 How many turns should be used to make the electromagnet?
4 Explain the shape of the graph.

Summary

The core of an electromagnet is made from iron. This is easily magnetised and loses its magnetism easily.

Questions

1 a Permanent magnets are made from steel rather than iron. Why?
b Explain why steel is unsuitable for electromagnets.
2 a Explain how the electric bell shown in Figure 7.2 works.
b Turning the contact screw makes the contact gap smaller. How does this affect the bell's action?
3 Figure 7.4 shows a design for an electrically operated lock.
a Explain what happens when the switch is closed.
b Why is the spring necessary?
c Why is the bolt made partly of iron and partly of aluminium?

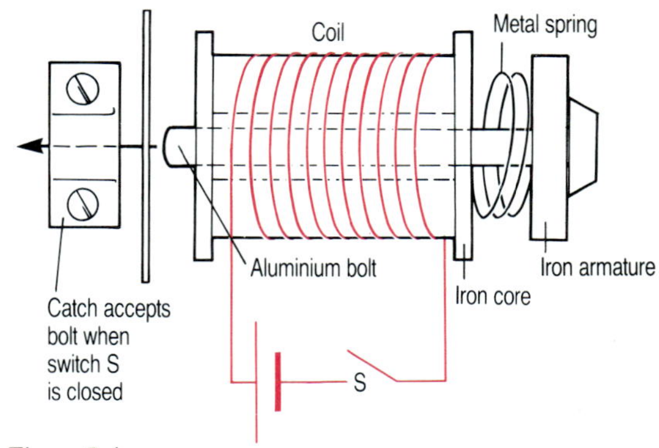

Figure 7.4

7.2 The electric motor

A simple electric motor consists of a coil of wire on a spindle, as shown in Figure 7.5. When current is passed through the coil, it turns. One side of the coil is pushed one way and the other side is pushed the other way.

● Why does this happen?

The current along each side of the coil produces a magnetic field. This interacts with the magnet's field. The current-carrying wires along each side are pushed by the magnetic field. This is called the **motor effect** (see Figure 7.6).

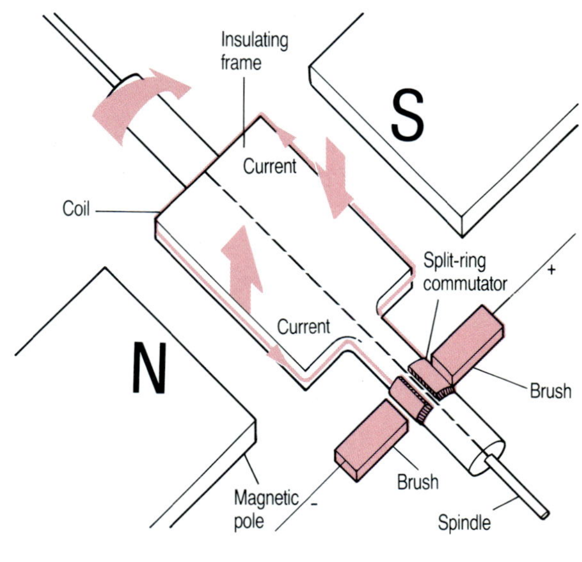

Figure 7.5 A simple electric motor

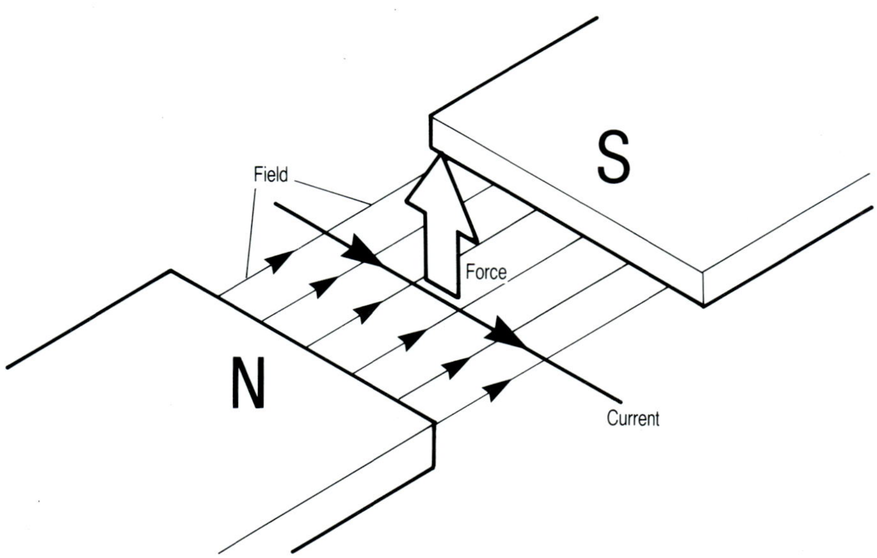

Figure 7.6 The motor effect

In Figure 7.5 the field tries to turn the coil clockwise. If the coil is turned through 180° without changing the current direction in the coil, the field tries to turn it back again, ie anticlockwise. To make the coil turn clockwise again, the current direction round the coil is reversed. This is the purpose of the **split-ring commutator** which connects the coil to the battery. This reverses the coil current every half-turn, making the coil spin in one direction only.

Activity 7.2

Make a model motor

Construct and test the model motor shown in Figure 7.5.
What is the effect of:

1 increasing the current
2 winding more turns on the coil
3 changing the magnet round
4 reversing the battery connections to the motor
5 winding the coil on an iron core?

How a motor works

Figure 7.7 shows an end-on view of the forces on the coil during one complete turn.

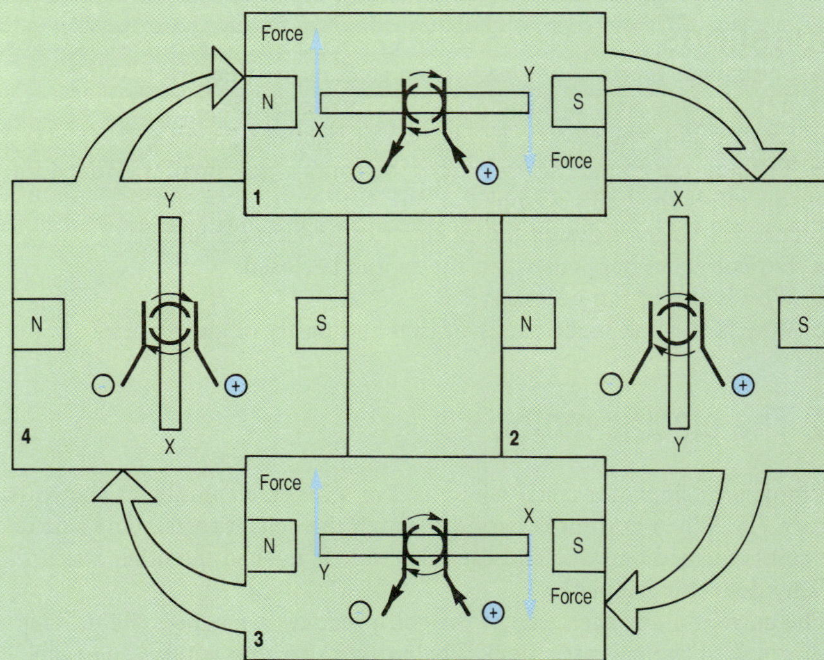

Figure 7.7 How a motor works

1 Current passes up side X and down side Y. The magnetic field pushes the coil clockwise, making it turn over.
2 When it has turned through 90°, the brushes disconnect from the coil. The coil's momentum carries it round.
3 The split-ring commutator now connects side X to the positive terminal of the battery. This reverses the current round the coil. Current now passes down side X and up side Y. This makes the coil continue turning in the same direction.
4 When the coil has turned through 270°, the brushes once again disconnect from the coil. The coil's momentum carries it round to position **1** again.

Figure 7.8 A practical motor

Summary

The motor effect is the force on a current-carrying wire in a magnetic field. The armature of an electric motor is pushed round continuously by the forces on its coil windings.

Practical electric motors

Food mixers, hair dryers, personal stereos, computer disc drives and electric drills are just a few appliances that contain electric motors. Figure 7.8 shows the **armature coils** of an electric drill. Several coils are wound on the armature core. Each coil is connected to a pair of contacts in the commutator. A multi-coil armature like this makes the motor turn more smoothly than if it had just one coil.

The motor in Figure 7.8 is fitted with an electromagnet in place of the usual permanent magnet. The voltage supply which provides the armature current is also used to supply the electromagnet current.

Questions

1 How would the performance of an electric motor be changed if
  a stronger magnets were used
  b more turns were wound on the coil?
2 a List ten appliances that each contain one or more electric motors.
  b A typical car contains several electric motors. Make a list of uses of electric motors in a car.
3 Claire and Jo have make a model electric motor with an iron armature core. The motor runs much faster and more smoothly than with a wooden block as the core. Why?
4 a In Figure 7.5, what would happen to the direction of rotation of the coil if
    i the battery connections were reversed
    ii the magnets were swapped over
    iii the battery connections and the magnets were reversed?
  b Explain why a motor with an electromagnet works using alternating current, but a motor with a permanent magnet does not.

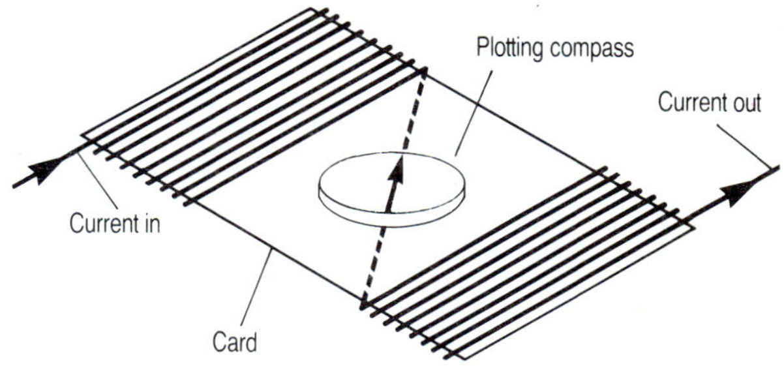

Figure 7.9 A plotting compass ammeter

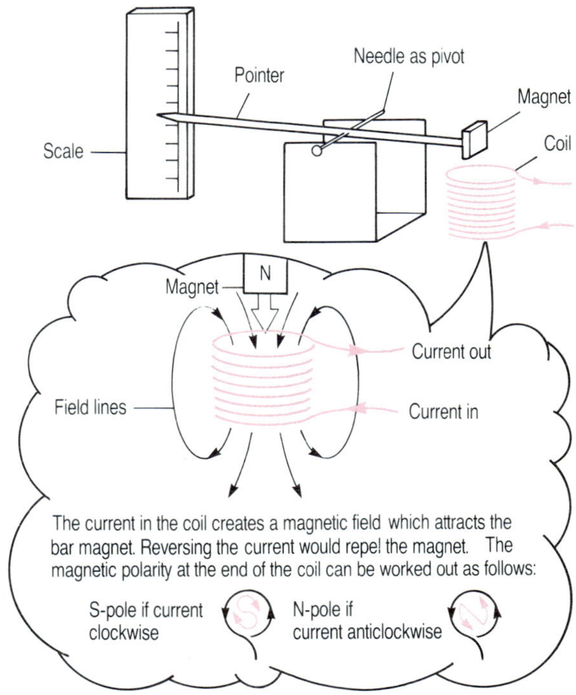

Figure 7.10 A moving-magnet ammeter

7.3 Make and test an ammeter

Andre Ampère was the scientist who first investigated electric currents. He and other scientists used magnetic compasses to detect and measure currents. Figure 7.9 shows how to make a simple ammeter using a plotting compass.

- To make the compass needle deflect, what orientation should the coil have?

If it is lined up along a north-south axis, it will not work very well.

- Why not?

Increasing the current from zero should make the compass needle gradually turn more and more away from magnetic north. This happens if the coil axis is east-west.

The plotting compass meter needs to be lined up correctly. Figure 7.10 shows a different way of measuring current using magnetic attraction. When current is passed through the coil, the bar magnet is pulled towards the coil. This happens because the current in the coil creates a magnetic field. As Figure 7.10 shows, the magnet is attracted by the coil.

- What would happen if the current direction was reversed?

The moving-coil meter

Moving-coil meters are widely used to measure current. They use the principle that a coil in a magnetic field turns when a current is passed through it.

Figure 7.11 shows how to make a model moving-coil meter. The springs return the coil back to its initial position when the current is switched off. The current enters and leaves the coil through the springs.

The construction of a practical moving-coil meter is shown in Figure 7.12. Unlike the model meter and the meters in Figures 7.9 and 7.10, the scale of this meter is **linear**. In other words, the deflection of the pointer is *proportional* to the current. On the meter scale, equal increases of current are spaced at equal intervals.

The scale is linear because of the iron drum. The drum makes the magnetic field **radial** as shown in Figure 7.12**b**. The field lines are therefore always along the coil plane, no matter how far the coil turns. Equal increases of current make the coil turn by equal amounts.

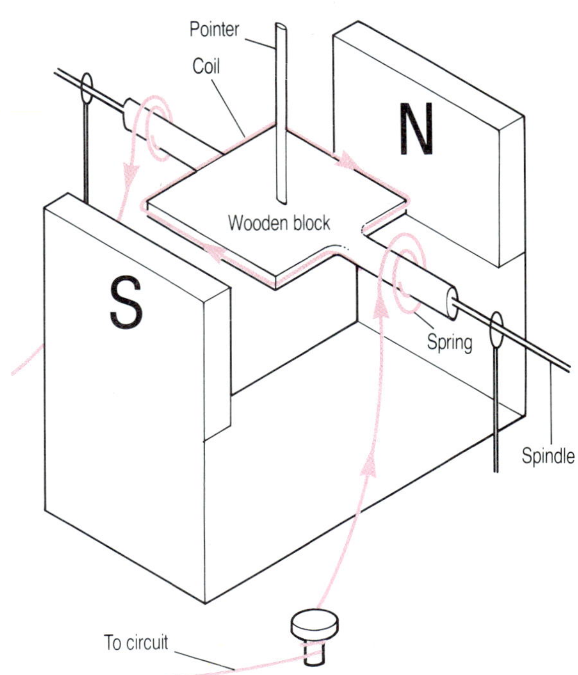

Figure 7.11 A model moving-coil meter

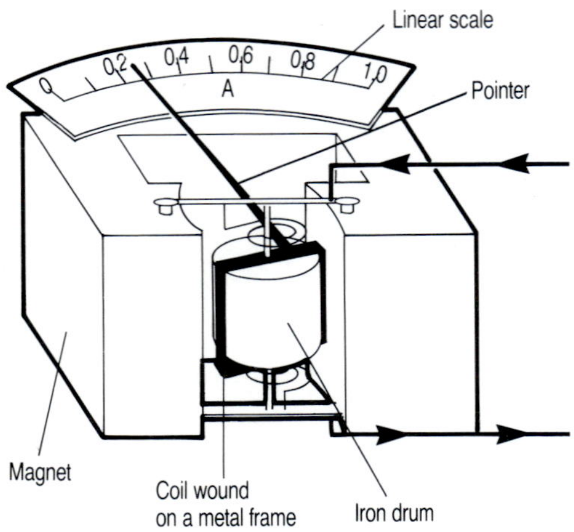

a *Construction*

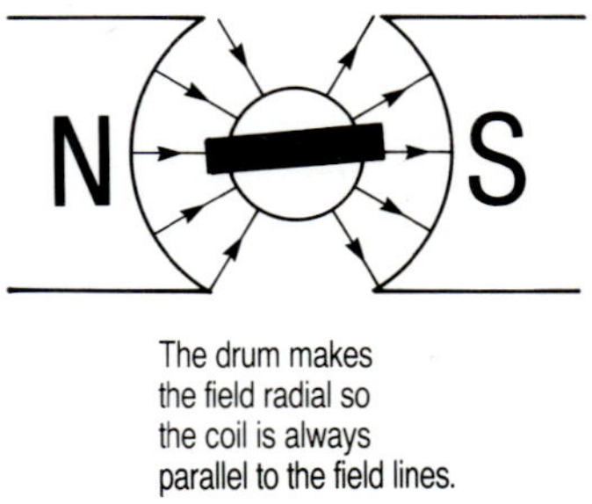

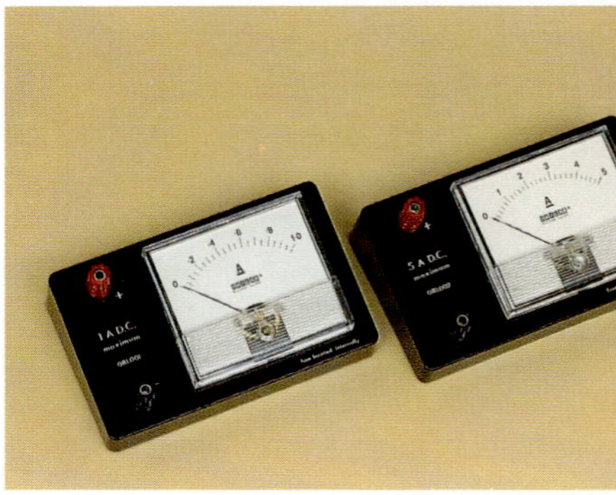

b *The radial field*

Figure 7.12 A practical ammeter

Activity 7.3

Make a moving-coil meter

1. Make a model moving-coil meter as shown in Figure 7.11.
2. Find out whether equal increases in current make the coil turn by equal amounts.
- Does the meter have a linear scale?
3. Connect your model meter in series with a battery and variable resistor. Vary the current and measure the maximum deflection.
- Would the pointer deflect more or less if
  - **a** you used a stronger magnet
  - **b** you wound more turns on the coil
  - **c** you made the springs tighter?

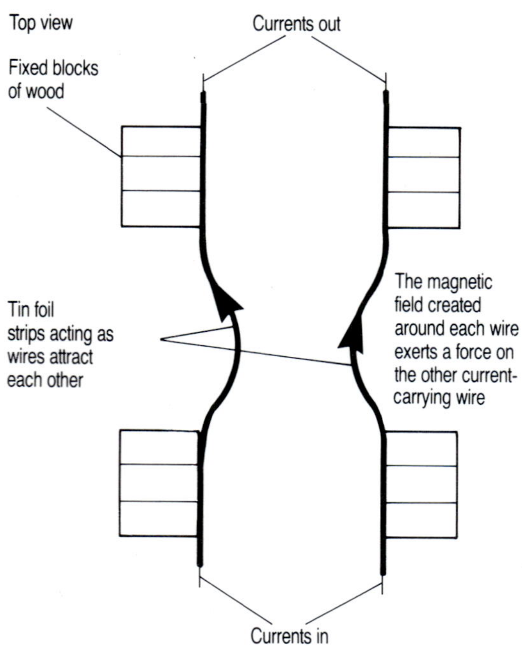

Figure 7.14 The force between two current-carrying wires

Digital meters

Digital meters (see Figure 7.13) do not use the moving-coil principle. They have no moving parts. The display is easier to read than a scale. The meter also responds faster than the moving-coil meter. However, it can easily be overloaded and damaged.

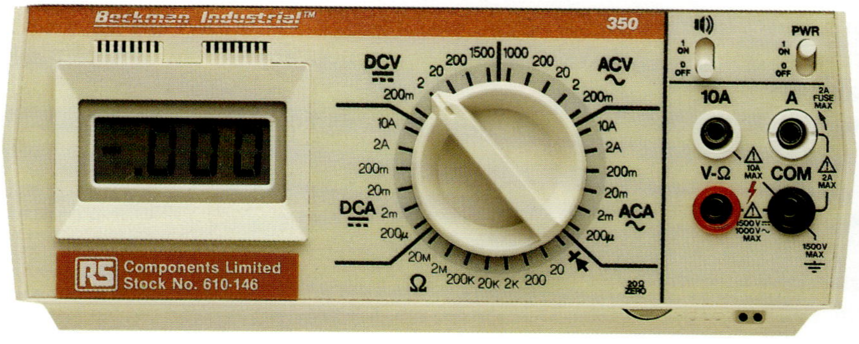

Figure 7.13 A digital meter

The ampere

Two parallel wires carrying current in the same direction attract each other. This happens because each current creates a magnetic field, and the fields interact. Figure 7.14 shows the idea.

- What do you think happens if the currents are in opposite directions?

The force between two parallel conductors carrying current is used to define the ampere. Imagine two very long, thin conductors exactly 1 m apart in a vacuum. They exert a force on each other. Connecting the conductors in series means the same current passes through them both. **One ampere** is defined as the current which causes a force of exactly 2×10^{-7} N on each metre of conductor.

Summary

The moving-coil meter has a linear scale. This means that the deflection of the pointer is proportional to the current.

Questions

1 a The deflection of the pointer of a model ammeter varied with current as shown by Table 7.2.

Deflection (mm)	0	21	54	82	90	55
Current (A)	0.00	0.17	0.26	0.46	0.61	0.75

Table 7.2

Use these results to plot a graph of deflection against current.

b How does the graph tell you that the pointer scale is non-linear?

2 Explain, with the aid of a sketch, how a moving-coil meter works.

3 Karen thinks it is possible to design a moving-coil meter with an electromagnet instead of a permanent magnet. Figure 7.15 shows her first design sketch.

a She reckons that passing current in either direction will make the pointer deflect in one direction only. Do you think she is correct? Explain your answer.

b She tests the meter in series with an accurate ammeter and finds its scale is non-linear.
What do you think makes the scale non-linear?

4 Two parallel wires carry current in opposite directions.

a Do the wires attract or repel each other?

b What would happen if they both carried alternating current?

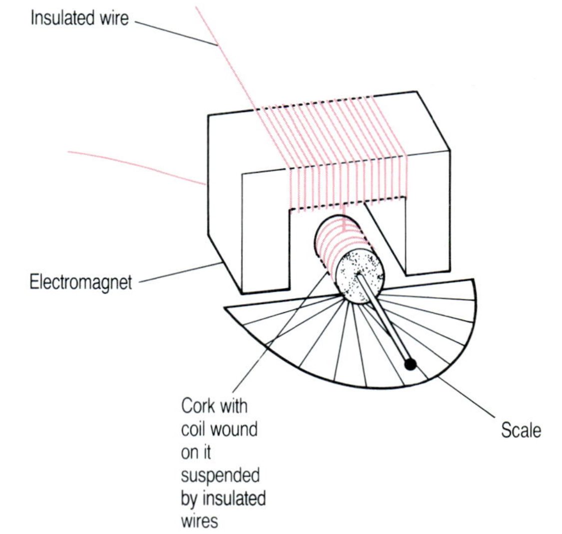

Figure 7.15

7.4 Electron beams

When you watch a television programme, the picture you see is built up by a beam of electrons inside the television set. The electron beam is controlled by signals from a television transmitter which are picked up by the set's aerial.

Figure 7.16 A television picture is made by an electron beam

The electron gun

The television screen is the flat end of a thick-walled glass tube. Inside the tube, a beam of electrons from an **electron gun** at the narrow end of the tube is directed at the screen (see Figure 7.17). There is a vacuum inside the tube. Light is emitted from the screen where the beam hits it. The beam is used to create a picture on the screen.

The electron gun consists of a wire filament and a metal anode. Current passed through the filament heats it and makes it glow. As a result, electrons inside the wire gain sufficient kinetic energy to leave the filament. This process is called **thermionic emission**.

Because the electrons are negatively charged the positive metal anode draws them off the filament into a beam. Figure 7.17 shows how this happens. Electron beams were called **cathode rays** by the scientists who first investigated them. This was because the electrons came from the cathode.

The anode voltage is a measure of the 'push' on the electrons. If the anode voltage is increased, the speed of the electrons in the beam is increased. This is because the electrons are attracted more strongly towards the anode when the anode voltage is increased.

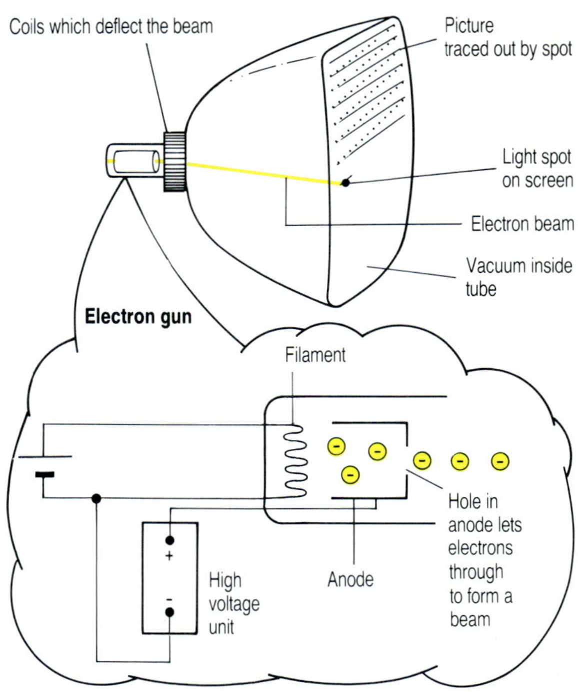

Figure 7.17 Inside a television tube

Using an electric field to deflect an electron beam

Using a special tube, as in Figure 7.18, a beam of electrons is passed between two oppositely-charged parallel plates. The voltage across the plates creates an electric field in the space between them. The beam is attracted towards the

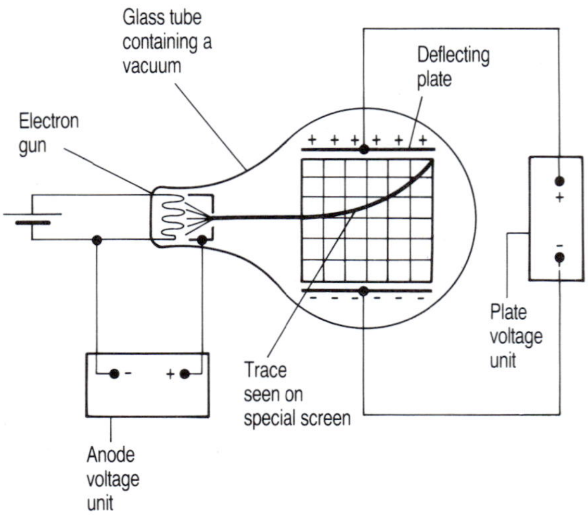

Figure 7.18 Tube construction

positive plate. This deflects the beam from its original direction. The path of the beam can be seen on a special screen inside the tube.

If the voltage between the two plates is increased, the deflection is made larger. If the anode voltage is increased, the deflection is made smaller. This happens because the electrons travel faster and so spend less time between the plates.

Activity 7.4

Using an oscilloscope

An **oscilloscope** is an electron tube that is used to display electrical signals. Connect a microphone to an oscilloscope (see Figure 7.19). Whistling a steady note near the microphone produces a steady waveform on the screen. Try different sounds.

Figure 7.19 Displaying waveforms

How an oscilloscope works

An oscilloscope screen is the flat end of a glass tube (see Figure 7.20). Inside the tube, an electron gun aims a narrow beam of electrons on to the flat end. The beam passes between two pairs of deflecting plates, then hits the screen where it produces a spot of light.

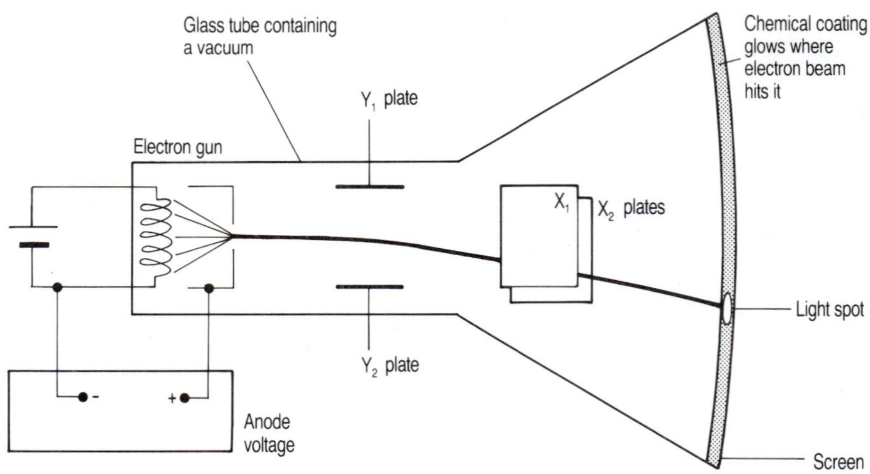

Figure 7.20 Inside the oscilloscope

The signal to be tested is applied to the Y-deflecting plates. This makes the spot on the screen deflect vertically. At the same time, a control signal, the **time base voltage**, is applied to the X-deflecting plates. This makes the spot move steadily across the screen. The result is that the spot traces out a pattern on the screen showing directly how the voltage applied to the Y-plates varies with time.

Magnetic deflection

The electron beam in Figure 7.18 can also be deflected using a magnet, as in Figure 7.21. Turning the magnet round pushes the beam in the opposite direction.

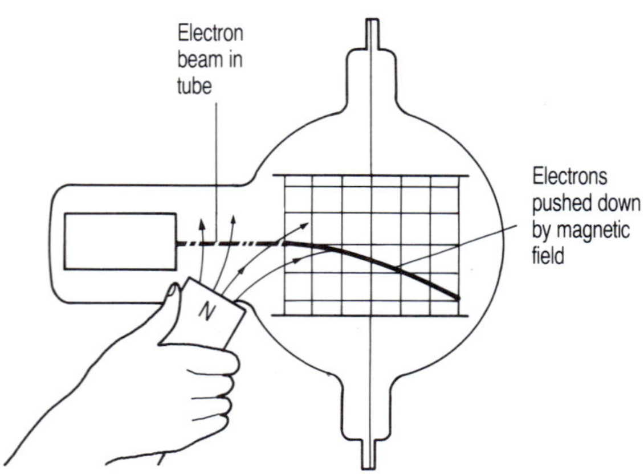

Figure 7.21 Magnetic deflection

The magnet can be replaced by an electromagnet. Varying the amount of current passing through the coil of the electromagnet controls the deflection of the electron beam. This is how electron beams in a television tube are controlled.

The television signal varies the brightness of the spot on the screen. The picture on the screen is built up as the spot travels repeatedly across the screen. Figure 7.22 shows how a black-and-white television picture is built up.

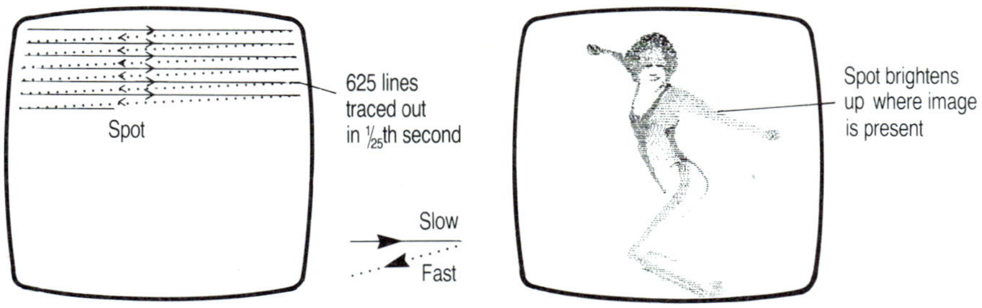

Figure 7.22 Building up the picture

Summary

An electron beam can be deflected by an electric field or a magnetic field. Oscilloscopes and television sets contain a vacuum tube in which an electron beam is produced and used to build up a display or picture.

Questions

1 a In the electron gun shown in Figure 7.17, why must the anode voltage be positive?

b An electron beam cannot be produced in an air-filled tube. Why?

2 In Figure 7.18, sketch the trace seen on the screen when

a there is no voltage between the deflecting plates

b the top plate is positive and the bottom plate is negative

c the top plate is negative and the bottom plate is positive.

3 Figure 7.23 shows some different oscilloscope traces. Which trace is produced when each of the following is connected to the input terminals of an oscilloscope

a a battery

b a microphone picking up a steady note of sound

c a microphone picking up noise

d a square wave generator?

4 In Figure 7.21, how would the trace on the screen be affected if

a a stronger magnet was used

b the magnet was turned round

c an electromagnet carrying alternating current was used in place of the magnet?

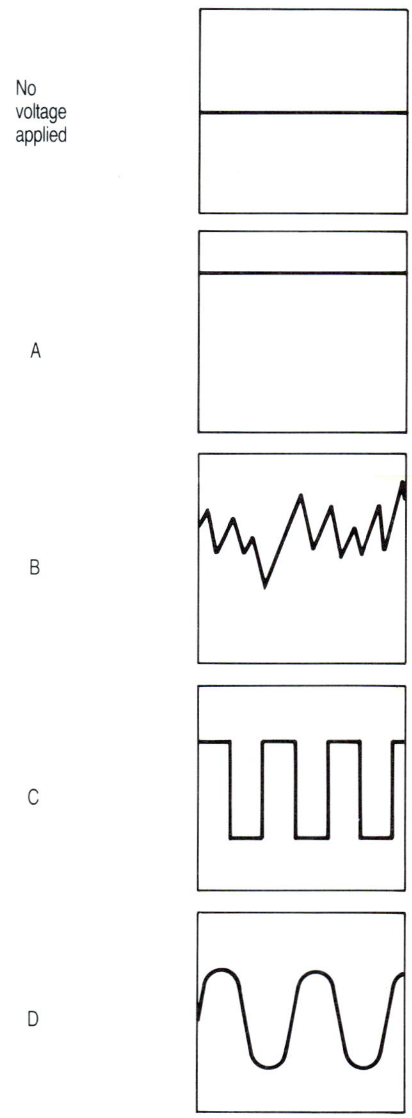

Figure 7.23

Unit 8

The electricity supply industry

8.1 The dynamo effect

A generation problem

An electric current produces a magnetic field. Can a magnetic field produce an electric current? This question was investigated by scientists for some years until Michael Faraday (see Figure 8.1) discovered the answer in 1831.

Faraday showed how to generate electricity using a magnet and a coil. He connected a coil to a meter. When he moved a bar magnet in and out of the coil, the meter pointer deflected. The movement of the magnet in and out of the coil was producing electric current. This is called the **dynamo effect**.

Faraday's work led to the invention of the **alternating current generator** which is used in power stations to generate electricity. He also invented the **transformer**, a vital piece of equipment for supplying alternating current to homes and factories.

Michael Faraday's discoveries about electromagnetism laid the foundation for our present-day electricity industry. After giving a lecture on his work, Faraday was asked what use this work might be. He replied 'What use is a baby?' No one can tell where new discoveries may lead.

Figure 8.1 Michael Faraday (1791–1867)

Activity 8.1

Investigating the dynamo effect

Connect a long length of insulated wire to a meter. Try the following tests (see Figure 8.2).

1 Move the wire across the lines of the magnetic field of a horseshoe magnet.

- Does the meter pointer move?

Move the wire back again.

- What difference does this make?

2 Make the wire into a coil and move the coil across the magnetic field in different directions and speeds.

- How can you make the pointer deflect as much as possible?

3 Keep the coil fixed and move the magnet around.

- What difference does this make?

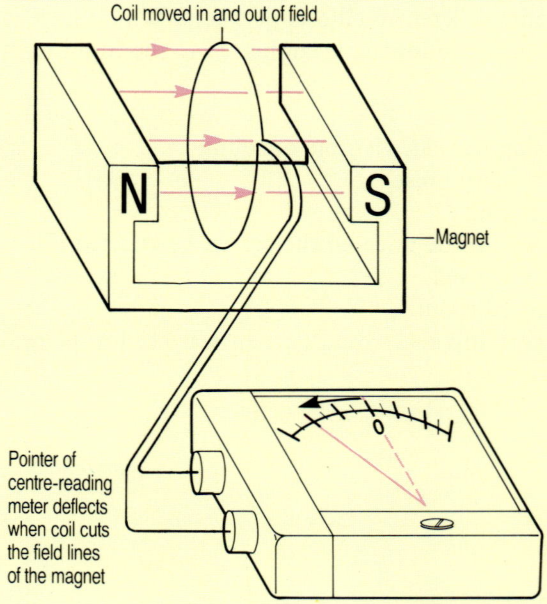

Figure 8.2 Making electricity

The tests in Activity 8.1 will show you that moving either the magnet or the wire produces an electric current. Electrons are pushed round the coil circuit when the magnet moves in relation to the wire. The magnet is said to **induce** a voltage in the wire. The process of using a magnet to induce a voltage in a coil is called **electromagnetic induction**.

In Figure 8.2, the wire is part of a complete circuit. The electrons are pushed round the circuit so an induced current is generated. If the circuit was broken, an induced voltage would still be created, but no induced current could pass round the circuit.

Energy changes

When a bar magnet is pushed into a coil connected to a meter, the meter pointer deflects. This happens because current is induced in the coil circuit. Work done by pushing the magnet into the coil produces electrical energy.

The induced current in the coil creates a magnetic field in the coil. This field acts against the incoming bar magnet. The field in the coil is like that of a magnet with an **induced pole** at either end of the coil. The induced pole acts against the bar magnet moving in. For example, if a N pole is pushed into the coil, the induced pole is also a N pole because this acts against the incoming pole. See Figure 8.3. This is an example of **Lenz's Law** which states that the direction of the induced current always acts against the change that creates it.

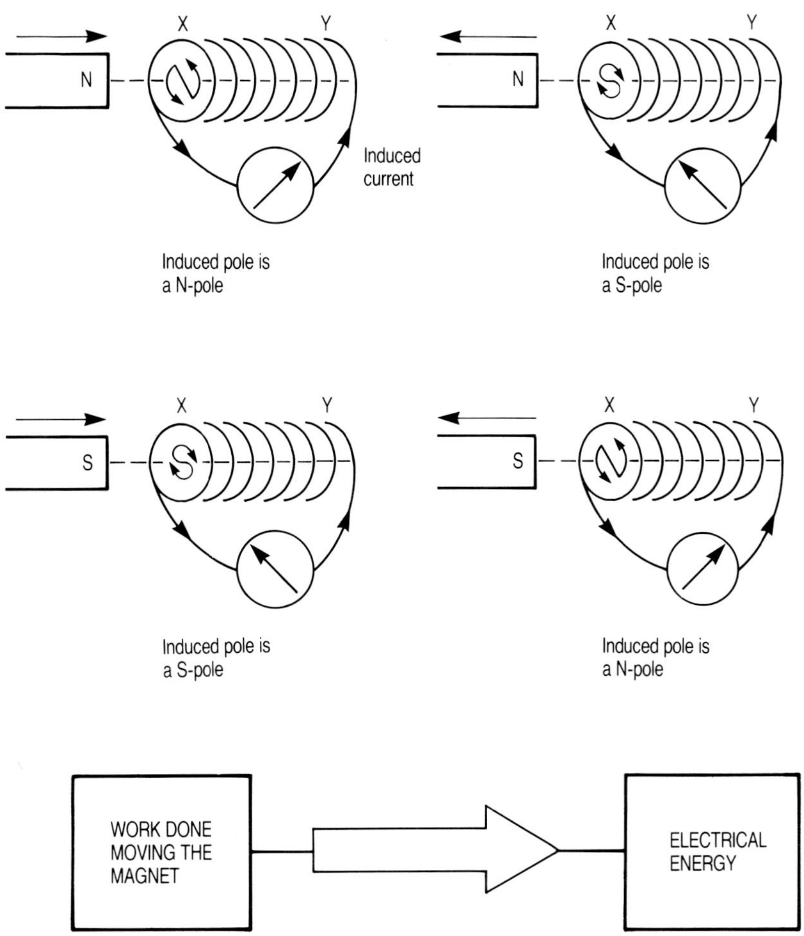

Figure 8.3 Induced current directions

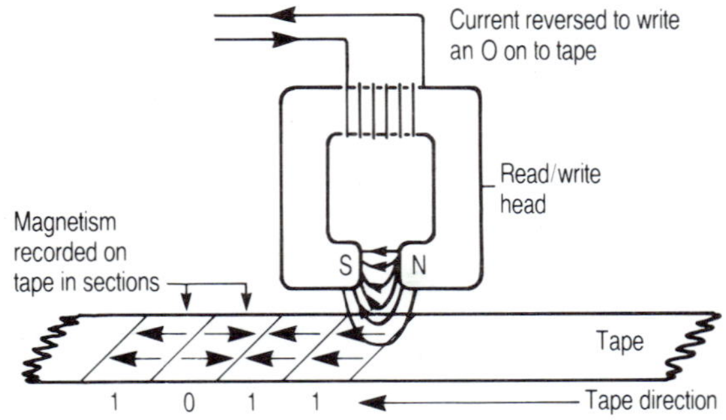

a *Writing on to the tape*

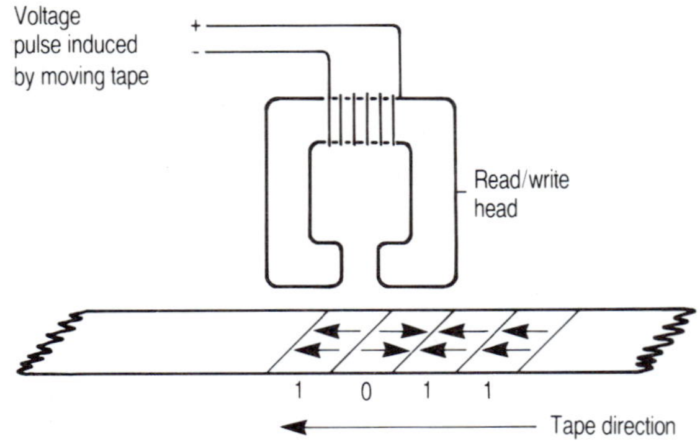

b *Reading the tape*

Figure 8.4 Using magnetic tape

Application:

Magnetic recording

Computers store information on magnetic discs and tapes. Information is handled by computers in the form of **bits** which are electrical signals representing the binary digits 1 and 0. Figure 8.4 shows how you could store the binary number 1011 on a magnetic tape. The tape is magnetised in opposite directions to represent binary 1 and 0.

Computer discs are used to store and retrieve huge amounts of information very rapidly. A single computer disc can store much more information than this book holds. A computer can read from discs and write information on to them very quickly, very much faster than you can read or write. The discs used at present are magnetic.

- How does a computer read and write information onto a magnetic disc?

The disc is **formatted** (arranged into sections) and a **read/write head** transfers information between the disc and the computer. Discs are made of plastic and coated with a magnetic film.

Summary

Moving a magnet relative to a coil induces a voltage in the coil. The faster the motion, the greater the induced voltage.

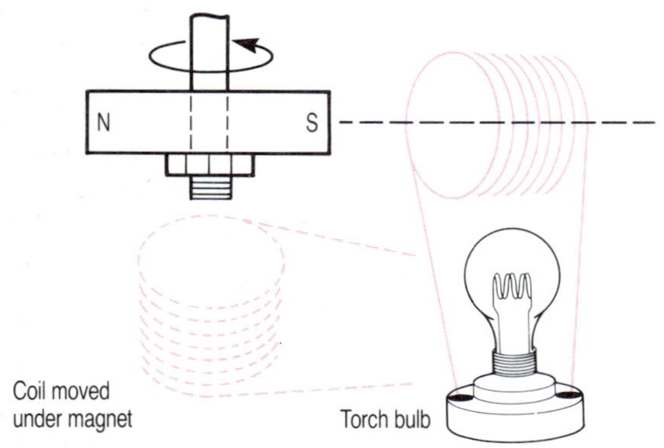

Figure 8.5

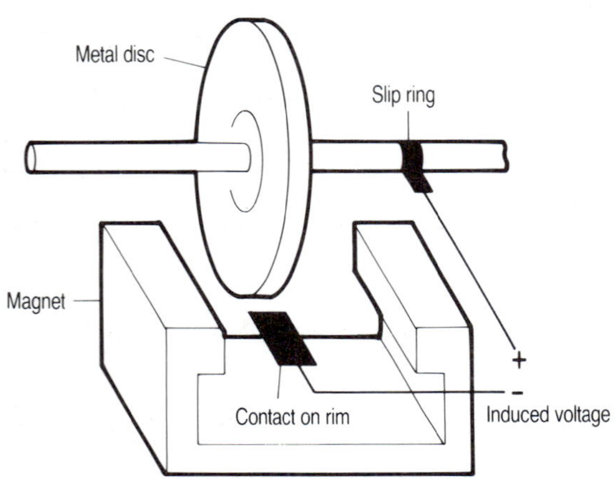

Figure 8.6

Questions

1 In Figure 8.3, what is the induced polarity at end X of the coil when
  a the N pole of a bar magnet is pushed into end X of the coil
  b the S pole of a bar magnet is pushed into end X of the coil
  c the S pole of a bar magnet is pulled out of end X of the coil?

2 Tim and Corrine have designed a dynamo, shown in Figure 8.5.
  a When the magnet turns, the torch bulb just glimmers. How could they make the torch bulb light up more without having to make the magnet turn faster?
  b Tim thinks it would be a good idea to place the coil under the magnet, as shown in Figure 8.5. Unfortunately, it doesn't seem to work when the magnet is turned. Why?

3 Faraday's disc generator consists of a metal disc that spins between the poles of a magnet, as in Figure 8.6. The motion of the disc pushes electrons to the edge of the disc, away from the centre. A voltage is induced between the centre and the rim of the disc. A meter is connected between the rim and the centre. The meter shows a steady reading if the disc turns at a steady rate.
  a What do you think happens if the speed is increased?
  b What do you think happens if the disc is turned in the opposite direction?

4 A bicycle is fitted with a dynamo to power its lamps.
  a Outline the energy changes in the dynamo and lighting circuit when the bicycle is ridden with its lamps on.
  b Why is it harder to pedal the bicycle when the lights are on?
  c How does the brightness of the lamps change if the cyclist goes faster?

5 a Explain how information is written on to a computer disc.
b When information is read from a computer disc, the read/write head scans over the disc surface. Why does this produce voltage pulses in the coil of the head?
c Video and audio cassettes contain magnetic recording tape. Why do you think programmes stored on tape gradually deteriorate?

8.2 Alternating current

When you switch on a light at home, **alternating current** passes through the light bulb. Alternating current (ac) repeatedly reverses its direction. In a light bulb connected to the mains, the current revolves in one direction and changes back again 50 times every second.

The alternating current generator

Main electricity is produced in power stations by alternating current generators. These generators are powerful machines, designed to convert the energy from fuel into electrical energy.

A simple ac generator is shown in Figure 8.7. It consists of a coil that is turned in a magnetic field. The coil is connected to a centre-reading meter via two slip rings.

When the coil is turned steadily, the meter pointer deflects first one way, then the opposite way, then back again. This carries on as long as the coil is kept turning. The current through the meter is an alternating current.

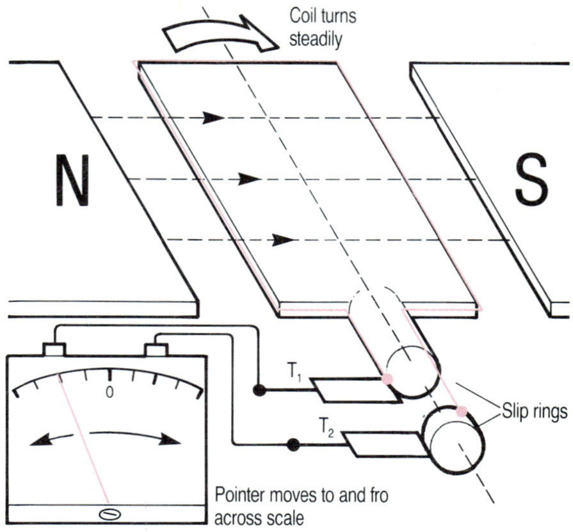

Figure 8.7 The ac generator

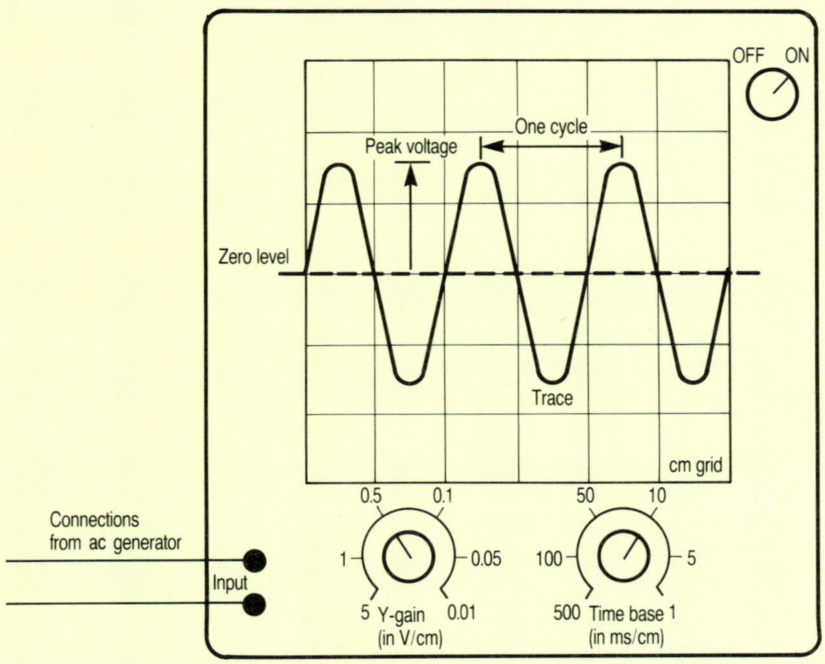

Figure 8.8 Using an oscilloscope

a *Working out the frequency: one cycle measures 2.0 cm across the screen. The time base is set at 10 ms/cm so one cycle takes 20 ms (= 0.02 s). The frequency is the number of cycles per second. This is 50 Hz (=* $\frac{1}{20}$ *s).*

b *Working out the peak voltage: The peak of the trace is 1.5 cm above the middle (i.e. zero level). The Y-gain is set at 0.5 V/cm. Therefore the peak voltage is 0.75 V (= 0.5 V/cm × 1.5 cm).*

Activity 8.2

Investigating the ac generator

1 Connect an ac generator to a centre-reading meter. Turn the coil at a steady speed and observe the movement of the pointer. The pointer vibrates about the zero mark on the meter scale.
- What happens if the coil is turned faster?

2 Use an oscilloscope instead of the meter (see Figure 8.8). The oscilloscope shows how the voltage across the generator terminals varies with time. The voltage changes polarity every time the coil makes half a turn. This is shown by the trace on the oscilloscope screen.

The maximum voltage is called the **peak voltage**.

The time for one complete cycle is the same as the time for one complete turn of the coil.
- What happens to the trace if the coil is turned faster?

3 Connect the oscilloscope to the terminals of a low voltage ac power supply unit. The trace is a **sine wave**. It is produced by a generator in a power station.

The **frequency** of an alternating voltage is the number of complete cycles per second. It is measured in **hertz** (Hz) where 1 Hz equals one cycle per second.

4 Work out the frequency of an alternating voltage displayed on an oscilloscope, as in Figure 8.8.

Figure 8.9 Power station generators

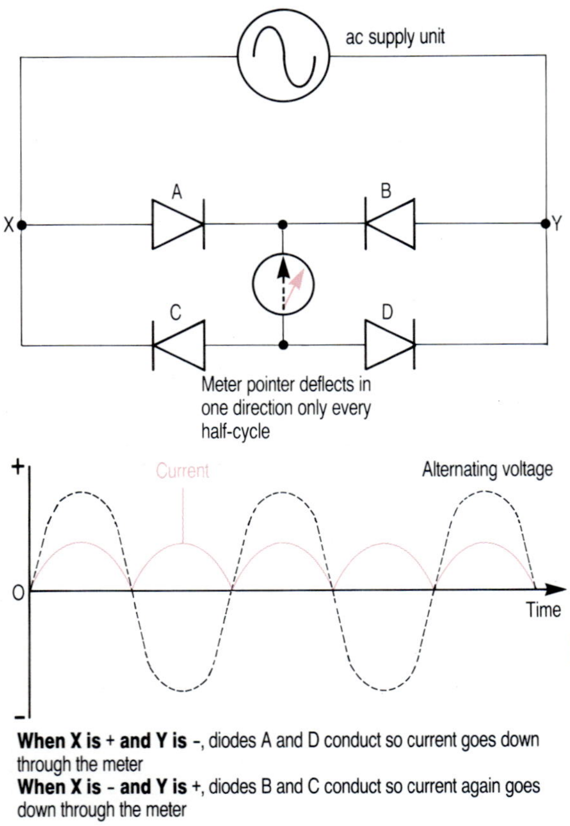

Figure 8.10 The bridge rectifier

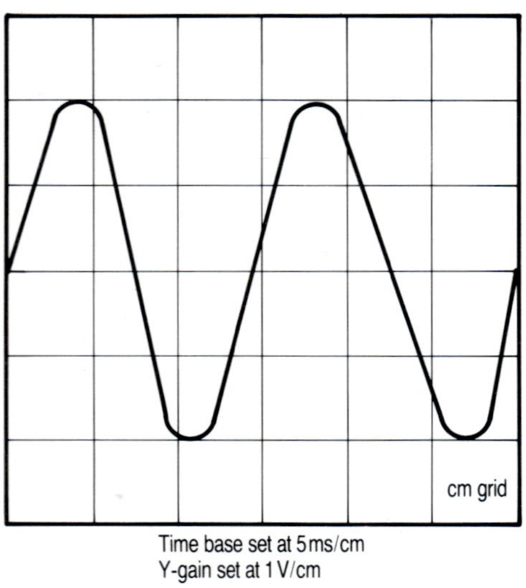

Figure 8.11

Power station generators

The huge generators in power stations (see Figure 8.9) are carefully controlled so they turn at a precise rate of 50 times each second. These generators are driven by steam turbines. Most power stations in Britain burn coal or oil to heat water to produce steam. Nuclear power stations use uranium to produce heat which is then used to make steam.

The peak voltage from a power station generator must not be allowed to increase. Otherwise, heaters and light bulbs would be overloaded and electric motors would turn too fast.

A typical power station generator produces a voltage of 25 000 volts. Mains electricity to homes and offices is supplied at 240 volts. **Transformers** are used to change the voltage from 25 000 volts at the power station to 240 volts at your home.

Converting alternating to direct current

Figure 8.10 shows how four diodes can be used to convert ac into dc. This circuit is called a **bridge rectifier**. The output current does not change direction when the alternating voltage changes polarity.

Summary

Electricity is supplied to our homes as alternating current. This is produced by generators in power stations.

Questions

1 Which of the following work on ac as well as on dc
  a a light bulb
  b a heater
  c a motor with a permanent magnet
  d a motor with an electromagnet instead of a permanent magnet?
2 With the aid of a diagram, explain how an ac generator works.
3 **a** Figure 8.11 shows an oscilloscope trace produced by an ac generator turning at steady speed. Work out the peak voltage and the frequency of the alternating voltage from the generator.
  b How will the trace change if the coil is turned at a slower speed?
4 **a** Daljit wants to measure the output voltage of an ac generator. He has a moving-coil voltmeter but his friend tells him it will not work with ac. Why?
  b Daljit thinks it is possible to measure the output voltage using a bridge rectifier with the meter. Sketch a suitable circuit diagram to show how this could be done.
  c In fact, the meter gives a steady reading which is less than the peak voltage from the generator. Why is the reading not equal to the peak voltage?
5 A hospital has a standby generator for use in emergency in case the mains supply fails. The generator is driven by a diesel engine.
  a Why is it necessary for a hospital to have a standby generator?
  b Outline the energy changes that take place when the generator is used to supply current for emergency lights in the hospital.

8.3 The National Grid

When you plug a heater into the mains, electricity is supplied to the heater. This electrical energy is generated in a power station some way from your home. It reaches you via a network of cables called the **National Grid**. These cables are often carried high above the ground by pylons.

The voltage from a power station generator is typically 25 000 V. The mains supply to your home from your local substation is 240 V. Between the power station and your home, the voltage is changed several times. This is done by **transformers**. Figure 8.12 shows where transformers are used in the National Grid.

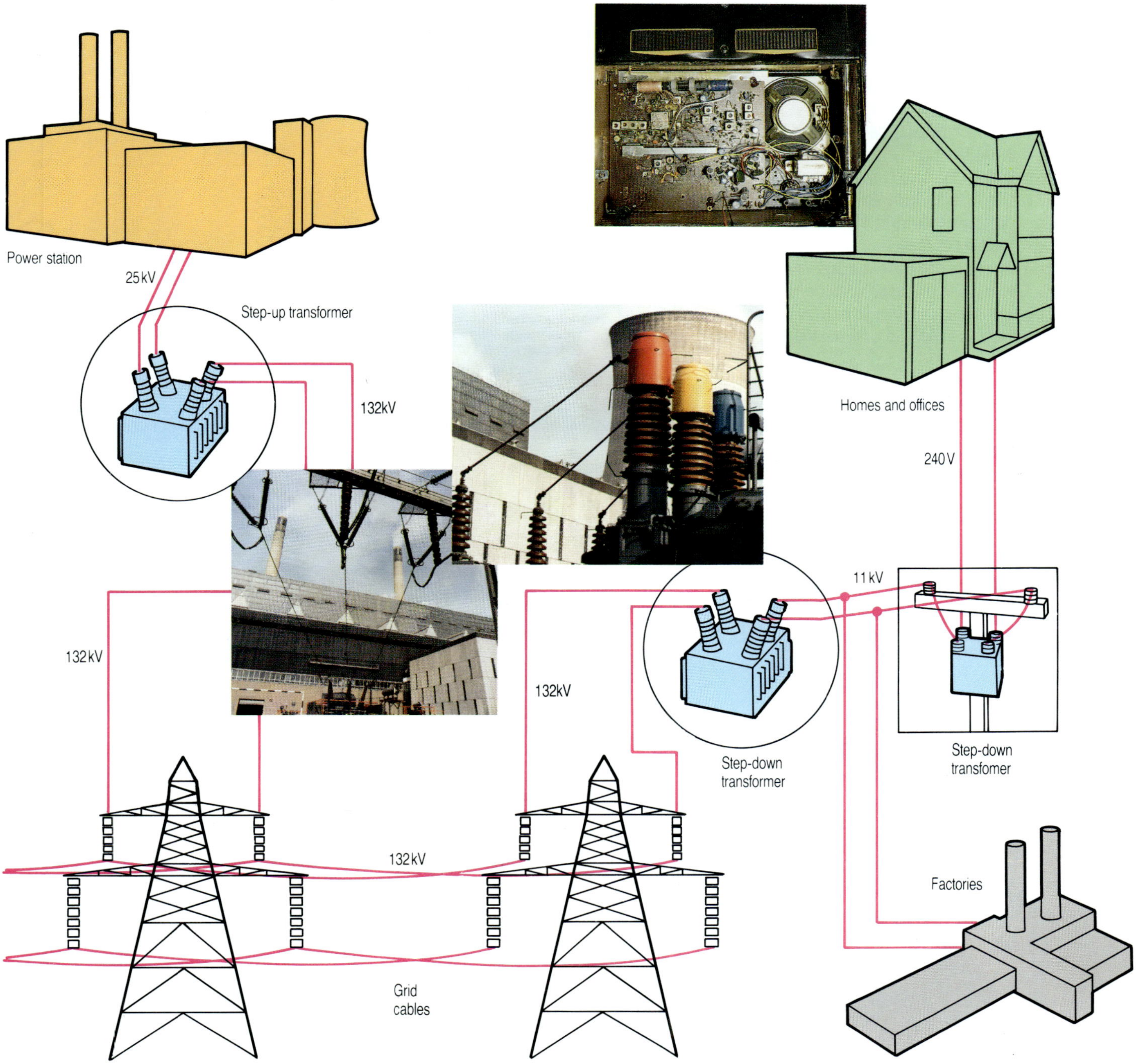

Figure 8.12 The National Grid

Activity 8.3

Investigating transformers

1 Wind a coil of insulating wire around a U-shaped iron core and connect the wire to a centre-reading meter. The meter deflects if a magnet is placed across the ends of the core.

- What happens when the magnet is removed?

2 Replace the magnet with an electromagnet (see Figure 8.13). Make the electromagnet using another iron core and some wire. Put the two cores together. Connect the electromagnet in series with a battery and a switch (see Figure 8.14).

- What happens when the switch is closed?

Open the switch and see what happens.

The steel core becomes magnetised when the switch is closed. This has the same effect on the meter as placing a magnet on the core. The growth of magnetism in the first coil induces a voltage in it. The magnetism is lost when the switch is opened. This induces an opposite voltage.

Changing current in one coil induces a voltage in the other coil. This is called the **transformer effect**.

3 Replace the meter with a torch bulb and the battery with a low-voltage ac supply unit. Switch the supply unit on.

- What happens to the bulb?

This is a simple transformer. The coil connected to the supply unit is called the **primary** coil. The other coil is called the **secondary** coil.

- What happens if the two cores are separated?

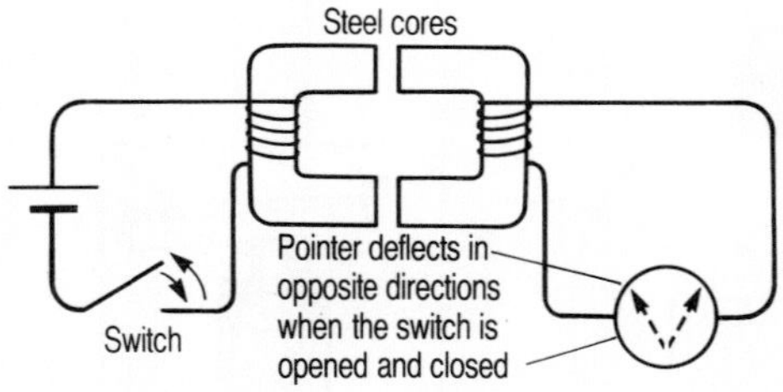

Figure 8.13 Using an electromagnet

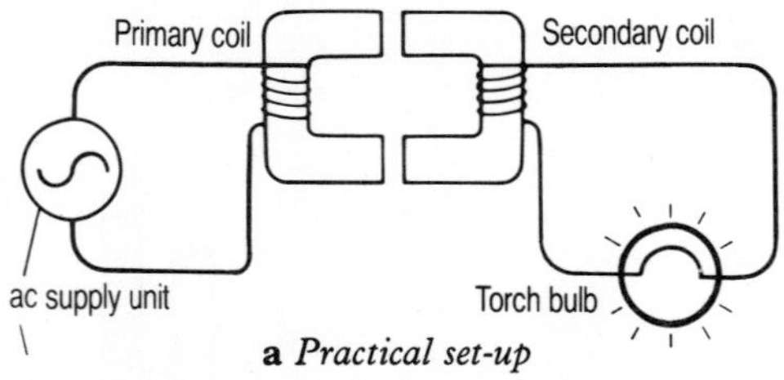

a *Practical set-up*

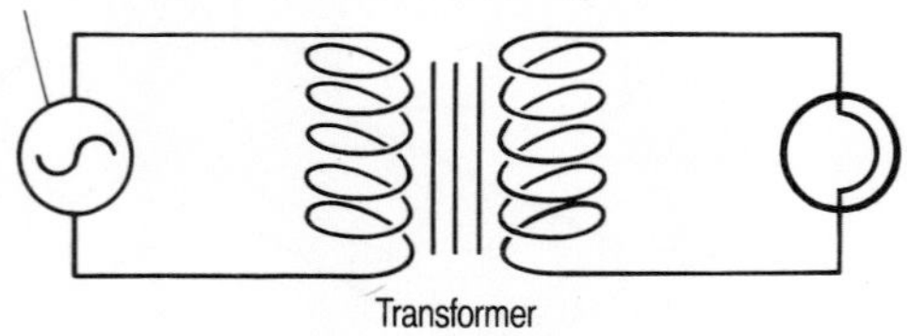

b *Circuit diagram*

Figure 8.14 The transformer effect

How a transformer works

Changing the current through the primary coil changes the magnetism of the steel core. This induces a voltage in the secondary coil, just as if a magnet was brought near the secondary coil.

If alternating current passes through the primary coil, the magnetism in the core alternates. This causes alternating voltage to be induced in the secondary coil.

Activity 8.4

Testing a model transformer

In Figure 8.14, winding more turns on the secondary coil makes the torch bulb brighter. The voltage induced in the secondary coil is increased by winding more turns on it. It can also be increased by increasing the primary voltage (ie supply voltage).

Replace the torch bulb with a suitable voltmeter (see Figure 8.15). Find out what the induced voltage depends on.

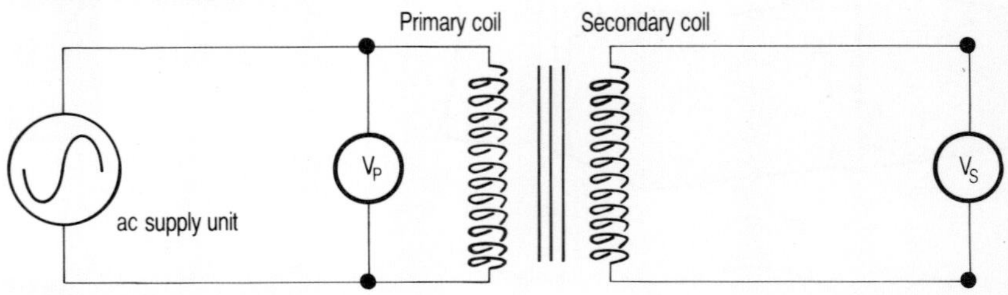

Figure 8.15 Measuring voltages

Table 8.1 shows some measurements from such an investigation.

Primary voltage (V)	**Primary turns**	**Secondary turns**	**Secondary voltage** (V)
1	20	20	1
2	20	20	2
2	20	40	4
2	40	40	2

Table 8.1

The measurements in Table 8.1 show that the secondary voltage is more than the primary voltage if there are more turns on the secondary than on the primary coil.

- Do your results agree?

The transformer equation

The secondary voltage in a transformer is given by the **transformer equation:**

$$\frac{V_s}{V_p} = \frac{N_s}{N_p}$$

where
V_s = secondary voltage
V_p = primary voltage
N_s = number of secondary turns
N_p = number of primary turns

Transformers are designed to step voltages up or down, according to the turns ratio.

- The **step-up transformer** has more turns on the secondary coil than on the primary coil. The secondary voltage is therefore larger than the primary voltage.
- The **step-down transformer** has fewer turns on the secondary coil than on the primary coil. The secondary voltage is therefore smaller than the primary voltage.

Transformers in the National Grid

Figure 8.12 shows step-up and step-down transformers used to supply electricity from the power station to your home. Step-up transformers are used to make the voltage on the power lines very high. This is because electrical power is transmitted much more efficiently at high voltage than at low voltage.

- Why is this?

Use the equation power = current × voltage to work out how much current is needed to supply 1 MW of power at 240 V. Then work out how much current is needed to supply the same amount of power at 132 000 V.

The higher the voltage, the smaller the current for the same power. So less energy is wasted due to resistance heating in the cables. The demonstration in Figure 8.16 shows that high-voltage transmission of electrical power is much more efficient than low-voltage transmission.

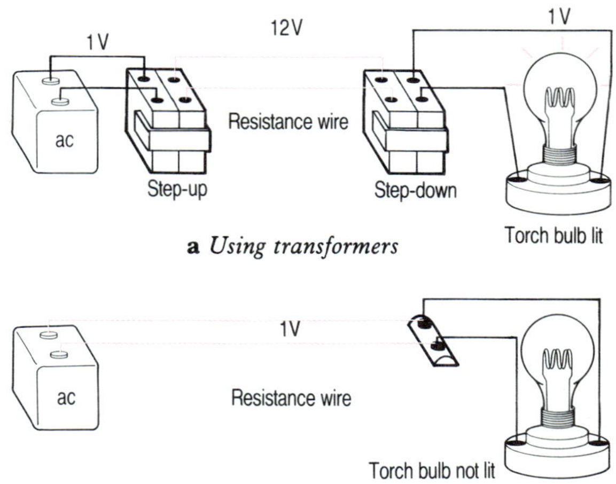

b *Without transformers*

Figure 8.16 A model power line

The efficiency of a transformer

Using high voltages to transmit electrical power would be pointless if the transformers used were inefficient.

- For every 100 W of electrical power supplied to a transformer, how much power does it deliver?

Figure 8.17 shows how this can be investigated using a model transformer.

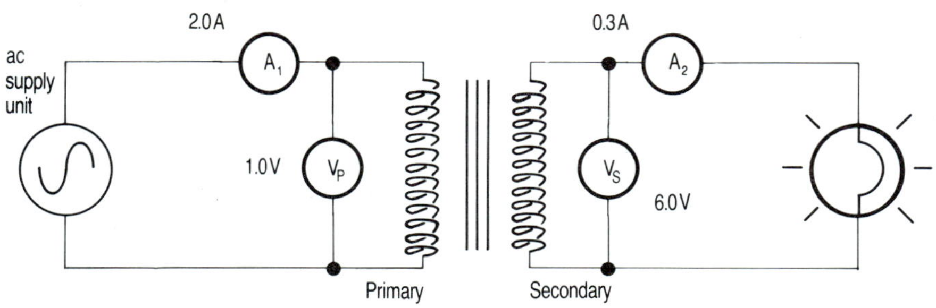

Figure 8.17 Transformer efficiency

The ac meters are used to measure the primary and secondary currents and voltages. Here are some typical measurments.

Primary voltage = 1 V
Secondary voltage = 6 V
Primary current = 2 A
Secondary current = 0.3 A

Power supplied *to* the transformer = primary current × primary voltage
= 2 A × 1 V = 2 W

Power supplied *by* the transformer = secondary current × secondary voltage
= 0.3 A × 6 V = 1.8 W

Work out the efficiency of the transformer using the equation:

$$\text{Efficiency} = \frac{\text{input power}}{\text{output power}} \times 100\%$$

The transformer in this example is 90% efficient. This means it wastes 10% of the power supplied to it and passes 90% on to the secondary circuit.

Activity 8.5

Pylons or underground cables?

The inhabitants of the picturesque Douglass valley are up in arms because the electricity company wants to build a power line on pylons through the valley. This would enable an old coal-fired power station, which has served the district for years, to be closed down. The valley dwellers want the power cables to be buried underground.

1. Burying the cables will cost more money than will be saved by closing the old power station. Give reasons for using underground cables, even though electricity consumers will have to pay more.
2. A valley farmer suggests that smaller pylons could be used. This would mean using a lower voltage on the cables. Why would this make the electricity more expensive to supply?
3. Summarise the options and explain which one you favour.

Summary

Transformers are used to step alternating voltages up or down. The network of cables used to transmit electricity from power stations to local substations is called the National Grid.

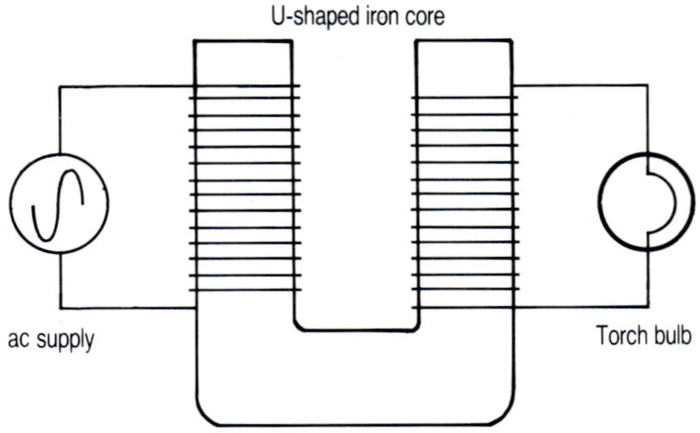

Figure 8.18

Questions

1 Figure 8.18 shows a model transformer made using two coils wrapped on a U-shaped iron bar.
- **a** The torch bulb can be made brighter by placing a straight bar across the ends of the U-shaped bar. Why?
- **b** Why does the torch bulb become dim if the secondary coil is slid off the U-shaped core?
- **c** If the coils were both wrapped on a straight iron bar, the torch bulb would be dim. Why?

2 **a** A low-voltage ac power unit contains a transformer that steps the voltage down from 240 V to 12 V. If the primary coil has 8000 turns, how many turns are on the secondary coil?
- **b** A 12 V, 24 W light bulb is connected across the terminals of the secondary coil. Work out the current in the secondary circuit.
- **c** If the transformer is 100% efficient, how much power is supplied to the primary coil of the transformer when the light bulb is connected across the secondary coil?
- **d** How much current then passes through the primary coil?

3 The cover photograph shows pylons holding 132 000 V cables in the air.
- **a** Why is the electric power carried along the cables at such a high voltage?
- **b** How is the voltage reduced to 240 V at the end of the power line?
- **c** Why must the cables be so high?
- **d** The cables are held from the arms of the pylon by means of glass or ceramic supports. Why are the supports made of glass or ceramic materials?

4 Before the National Grid was established, each town had its own electric power company. Some provided ac, some dc and the voltage differed from one town to another. The ac companies were able to supply electricity more cheaply because they could serve wider areas with more consumers.
- **a** Why were the ac companies able to supply electric power efficiently over long distances?
- **b** Why could the dc companies not do this too?

8.4 Electricity demands

At the end of a popular television programme, lots of people switch their electric kettles on to make a hot drink. The demand for electricity rises sharply within minutes.

- How much electric power is needed by one million 3 kW electric kettles?

Large power stations are capable of generating more than 1000 megawatts (MW) of power, but they can take hours or even days to bring into operation. The demand for electricity varies during each day and the operators of power stations have to match supply and demand.

We shall look at how this is achieved in North-west England and North Wales. This region operates the world's first **pumped storage** scheme to even out the demand for electricity. Figure 8.19 shows how the demand for electricity in the region varies during a typical day in summer and in winter. The major power stations in the region are shown in Figure 8.20. They supply electricity to the grid system which supplies the substations in the region.

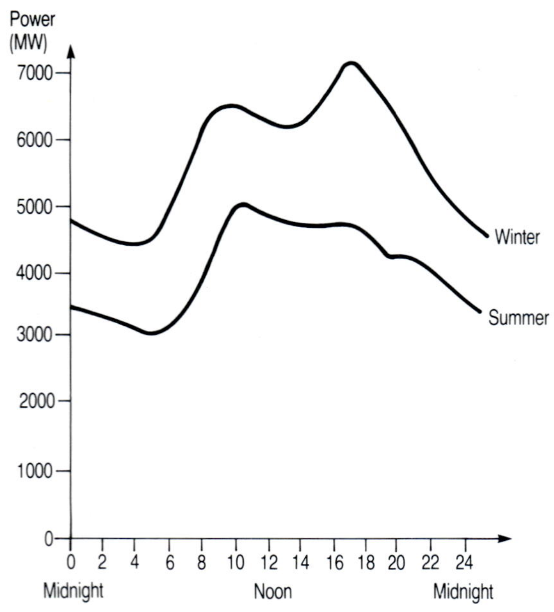

Figure 8.19 Electricity demand

Power stations in North-west England and North Wales

1 Coal-fired power stations can supply up to 2500 MW of electricity. They were built near coalfields. Some coalfields are now exhausted. If the boilers of a coal-fired power station are kept on standby, they can start to generate electricity within minutes.
   Britain has huge reserves of coal, enough to meet present needs for several centuries. Large coal-fired power stations have replaced many of the small 'local' stations.

2 Oil-fired power stations were built when the cost of oil was much lower than at present. The two oil-fired stations in the North West can supply up to 1100 MW. They are much more expensive than coal-fired stations. They can also be switched on within minutes if on standby.

3 Nuclear power stations supply up to 2500 MW at present. They take weeks to start up or stop so they are used to give a steady supply of power. Although they are much cheaper to run than coal- or oil-fired power stations, the cost of building a nuclear power station is much higher than for coal or oil. They have a lifetime of 30 years and the cost of taking nuclear power stations 'out of commission' is likely to be very high.

4 Hydroelectric power stations in North Wales make a total contribution of about 100 MW at very low cost. No fuel is needed because they generate electrical energy from the loss of potential energy when water runs downhill.

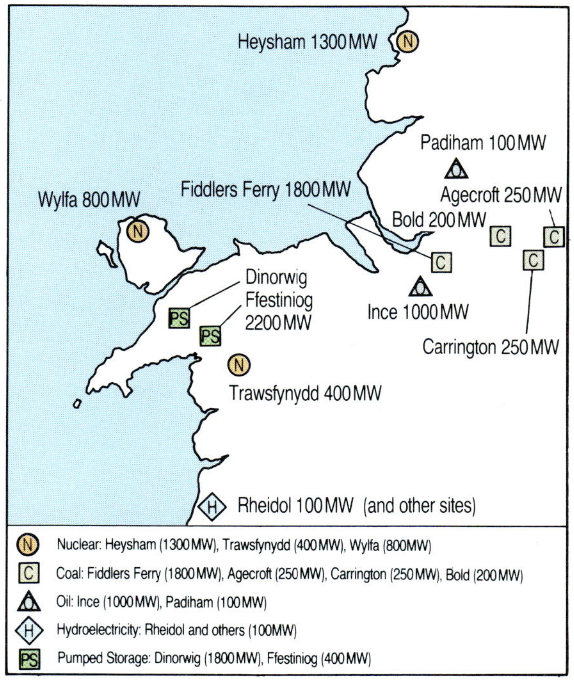

Figure 8.20 Power stations in North-west England and North Wales

Activity 8.6

A power game

Imagine you have the job of matching supply and demand in summer in North-west England and North Wales. You would not need to use all the stations.

- Which ones would you use?

The peak demand is about 5000 MW. This could be met by using all the nuclear power stations and all the coal-fired stations. However, meeting the peak demand in this way is inefficient because demand falls to about 3000 MW during the night.

Pumped storage stations at Dinorwig and Ffestiniog are designed to store energy produced by other power stations when demand is low. This energy is then used when demand is high. The two stations can supply 2200 MW. Figure 8.21 shows how they work.

- How does this help to match supply and demand?

The nuclear, hydroelectric and coal-fired stations could be used to generate 4300 MW at a steady rate. This is the **base load.**

- Would the energy stored when demand is lower than 4300 MW be enough to supply power when demand is higher than 4300 MW?

Perhaps the base load is too low.

Copy and complete Table 8.2 using Figure 8.22.

- Where would *you* draw the base load line in Figure 8.22?

Period of day	Demand	Supply – demand
0–4 am	3200 MW	+1100 MW
4 am–8 am	3000 MW	+1300 MW
8 am–noon		

Table 8.2

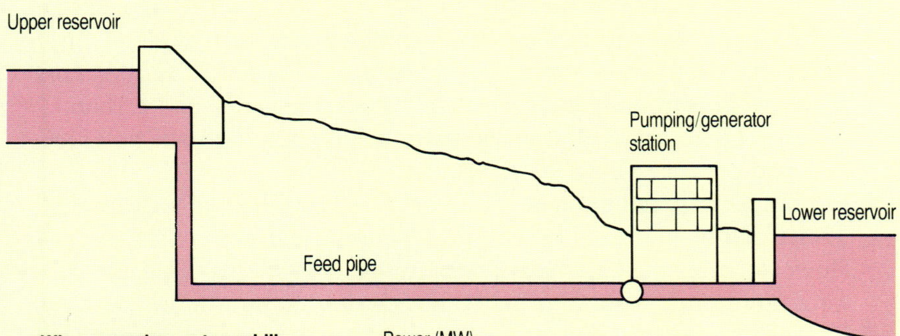

Figure 8.21 Pumped storage

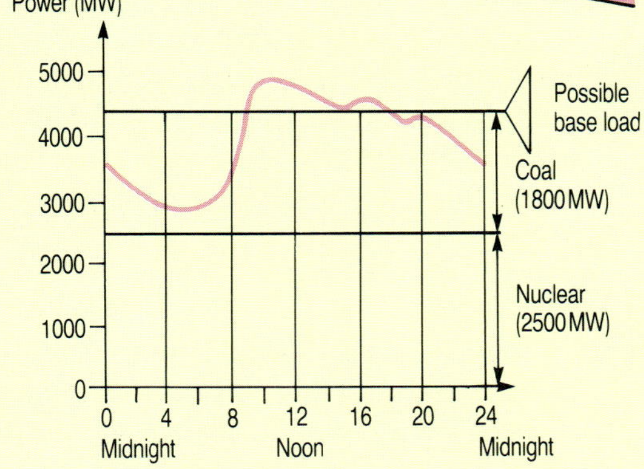

Figure 8.22 Matching supply and demand

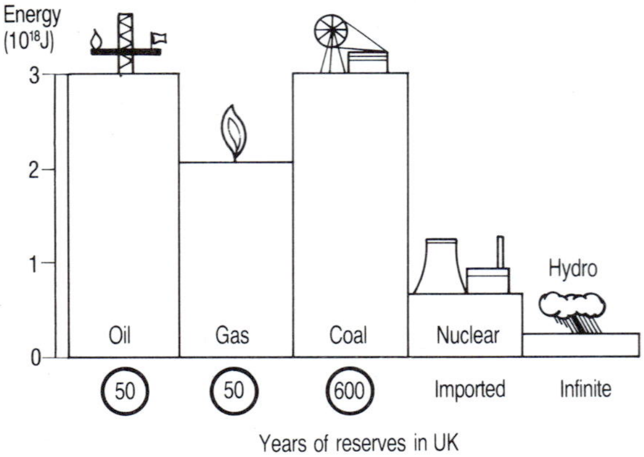

Figure 8.23 Annual fuel usage in the UK

Figure 8.24 A wind farm

Figure 8.25 Loft insulation

Activity 8.7

Dinorwig pumped storage scheme

Dinorwig is the largest pumped storage scheme in Europe. The upper reservoir (see Figure 8.21) is 500 m above the station. Its six reversible turbines take 6 hours to pump water from the lower reservoir to the upper reservoir. Each turbine needs 280 MW of electricity for this. When the flow is reversed, the water drives the turbines to generate electricity. Each turbine can generate 310 MW of electricity.

1 Outline the energy changes when **a** water is pumped uphill **b** water flows downhill through the turbines.

2 Work out the potential energy released when 1000 kg of water falls through 500 m.

$$\text{Change in potential energy} = mgh$$

where g = acceleration due to gravity, assume 10 N/kg
h = change in height

3 Each turbine can generate 310 MJ/s. What is the minimum mass of water that must flow through a turbine each second to provide this power output?

4 Each turbine needs 280 MW for 6 h and can produce 310 MW for 5 h. Use these figures to estimate the efficiency of a turbine.

Future needs

Planning for the future involves predicting supply and demand. Unpredictable events, like political changes in oil-rich countries, can ruin the best thought-out plans. Figure 8.23 shows Britain's annual fuel usage in the 1980s.

The demand for electricity is unlikely to decrease, judging from past trends. Oil reserves are limited and will probably run out within 50 years. Gas fields will probably be exhausted sooner. Gas and oil are likely to become more expensive if alternative fuels are not developed. The demand for electricity could rise considerably.

- What are the options to meet this increasing demand?

1 More coal-fired power stations could be built. However, burning coal produces **greenhouse gases** such as carbon monoxide and carbon dioxide. These cause **global warming** which may melt the polar ice caps and produce rising sea levels.

2 Nuclear power stations at present supply 20% of Britain's electricity. This could be increased by building more nuclear power stations. However, after the Chernobyl catastrophe in 1986, many people do not want more nuclear stations built, though they *do* want more electricity.

3 Renewable energy resources such as wind power, wave power and tidal power produce electricity without producing harmful waste products. A wind farm (see Figure 8.24) of 50 or more 20 MW aerogenerators could produce the same power as a 1000 MW station. Scientists think that renewable resources could supply more than 20% of our electricity needs, but much more development work is needed.

Save it!

In winter the demand for electricity rises, partly because we need to keep our homes warm. The equivalent of twenty 1000 MW power stations need to be switched on in Britain to meet our extra winter demand for electricity. Better insulation in homes and offices would reduce this extra demand considerably. Figure 8.25 shows one way of saving electricity.

- What other ways can you think of?

Power stations waste vast quantities of energy. A coal-fired power station generating 1000 MW of electrical power produces about 2000 MJ of heat per second. Its efficiency is about 33%. For every joule of electrical energy generated, two are wasted as heat.

Combined heat and power (CHP) stations are designed to generate electricity *and* to supply heat to local factories and offices. Figure 8.26 shows how a district CHP station reduces the overall demand for energy in the district. More CHP stations throughout Britain would reduce the demand for gas and oil for heating.

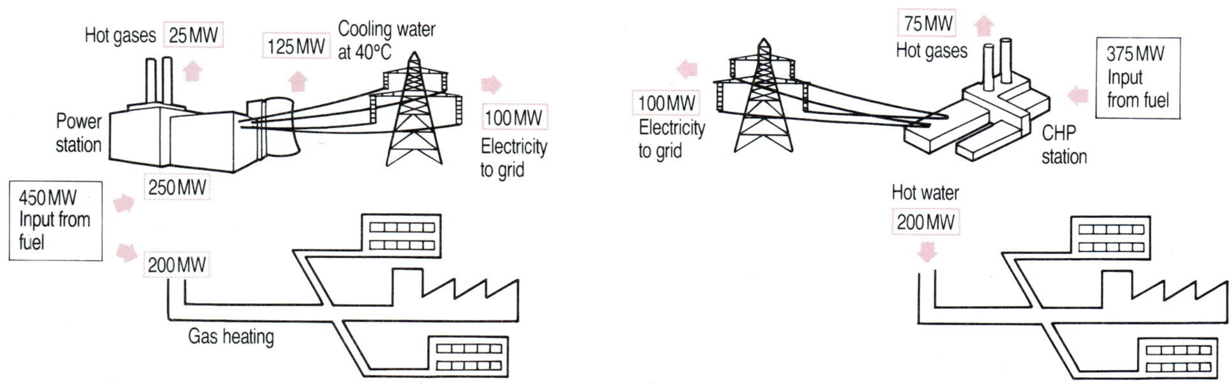

One non-CHP station can supply 100 MW of electricity. Heating at 200 MW is supplied by gas so the total input from fuel is 450 MW (= 250 MW for electricity + 200 MW for gas).

One CHP station can supply 100 MW of electricity *and* 200 MW for local heating. The input from fuel would be 375 MW.

Figure 8.26 The benefits of CHP

Questions

1 **a** Why is our demand for electricity higher in winter than in summer?
b Explain why the demand for electricity rises between 5 am and 9 am each day.

2 Figure 8.19 shows how the demand for electricity in North-west England and North Wales varies during one day in winter. How would you meet this demand, using the power stations and pumped storage schemes shown in Figure 8.20?

3 The demand for electricity in Britain could rise from 50 000 MW to 70 000 MW over the next 30 years.
a How many 2000 MW power stations would need to be built to meet this extra demand?
b Renewable resources could supply 20 000 MW of electricity. How many 2000 MW power stations would then need to be built if these renewable resources were developed?
c Present nuclear power stations are designed to last about 30 years. Replacement power stations will need to be built eventually. What type of power station do you think should be built? Explain.

4 **a** A CHP station is capable of producing 100 MW of electricity. 200 MJ/s of heat are carried away by cooling water. How many CHP stations would be needed to replace one 1000 MW power station?
b What would be the advantages and disadvantages of replacing a 1000 MW station with CHP stations in terms of
i energy efficiency **ii** the environment?

Summary

Increased demand for electricity can be met by building more nuclear and coal-fired power stations and by developing renewable energy resources.

Unit 9

Electromagnetic waves

9.1 The electromagnetic spectrum

In 1989, the spacecraft *Voyager 2* flew past the planet Saturn with its rings, a distance of 1400 million kilometres from Earth. The spacecraft sent pictures back to Earth that amazed the world (see Figure 9.1). Radio signals from a 20 W transmitter on the spacecraft carried the pictures.

Figure 9.1 Saturn's rings

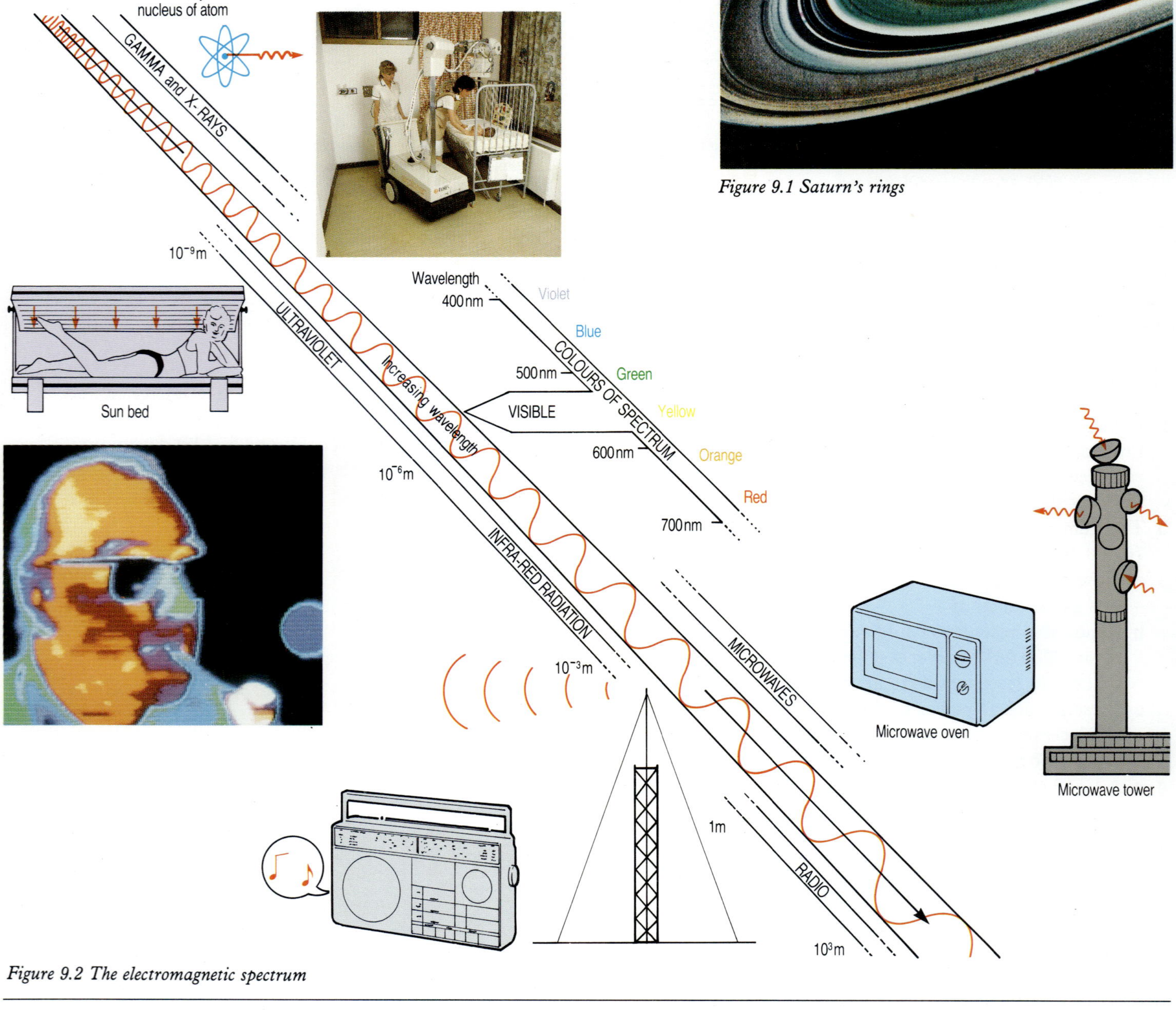

Figure 9.2 The electromagnetic spectrum

Radio waves are part of the spectrum of **electromagnetic waves**. Light waves are electromagnetic waves. Figure 9.2 shows the complete spectrum of electromagnetic waves. They all travel through space at a speed of 300 000 km/s. Their properties and uses depend on their wavelengths, which vary.

The electromagnetic spectrum – a fact file

1 Radio waves are emitted from transmitter aerials. Electrons in the aerial are forced to move up and down repeatedly, emitting the radio waves. When the waves pass across an aerial, they push electrons to and fro along the wire. This produces a detectable voltage in the wire. Radio waves cannot pass through metal sheets.
2 Microwaves are used for cooking and telecommunications. Food cooks much faster in a microwave oven than in a normal oven because the microwaves penetrate it. However, microwaves cannot pass through metal so food wrapped in tin-foil will not cook in a microwave oven. In telecommunications, microwave beams can carry much more information than telephone wires. Huge concave dishes are used to send and receive microwave signals.
3 Infra-red radiation is emitted by all objects. The hotter the object is, the more energy it emits. Ceramic cooker hobs emit mainly infra-red radiation from quartz halogen light bulbs. A typical cooker ring has four 500 W bulbs above a silvered reflector. This reflector directs most of the radiation upwards through the transparent hob.
4 Light is a small part of the electromagnetic spectrum. Our eyes cannot detect electromagnetic waves outside the visible range. Light beams in optical fibres can carry much more information than radio or microwaves.
5 Ultraviolet radiation is harmful to our eyes and skin. Solar radiation contains ultraviolet as well as visible radiation. The ultraviolet radiation in sunlight tans the skin, but too much can blister the skin or even cause skin cancer. Users of sunbeds should never exceed the exposure times recommended by the manufacturer.
6 X- and γ-radiation cover the same range of the electromagnetic spectrum and have similar properties. However, X-radiation is produced by X-ray tubes and γ-radiation is produced by radioactive isotopes.

9.2 Using electromagnetic waves

If you choose to go on work experience to a hospital, you will find electromagnetic waves in use in different departments. For example, **sunlamps** are used in the baby unit to cure jaundice. Fibre-optic devices called **endoscopes** are used to see inside the body. **Brain scanners** are designed to detect tiny radio signals emitted from hydrogen atoms inside the body. **X-ray machines** take pictures of internal organs (see Figure 9.3).

The X-ray department is one of the busiest places in a hospital. X-ray machines are operated by specially trained staff called **radiographers**. X-radiation is harmful so great care has to be taken when operating X-ray machines. Radiographers have to know how the X-ray machines work and what effect X-rays have on the body.

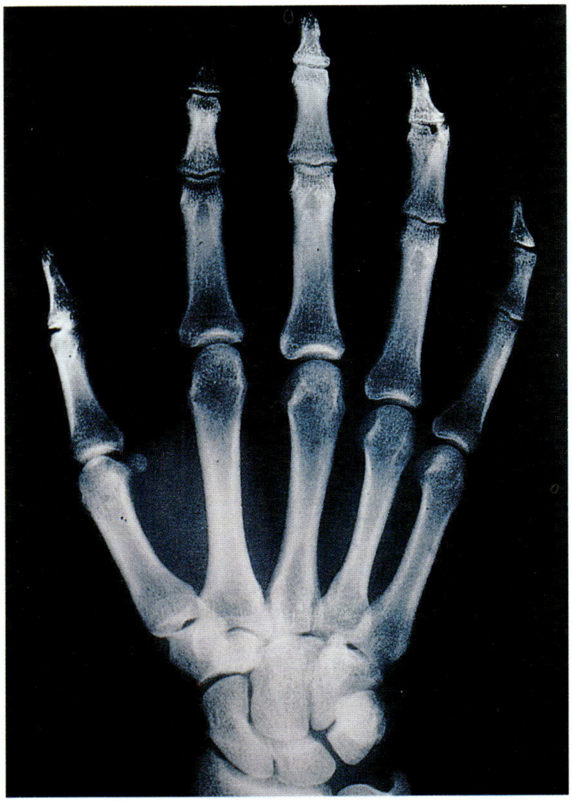

Figure 9.3 An X-ray picture

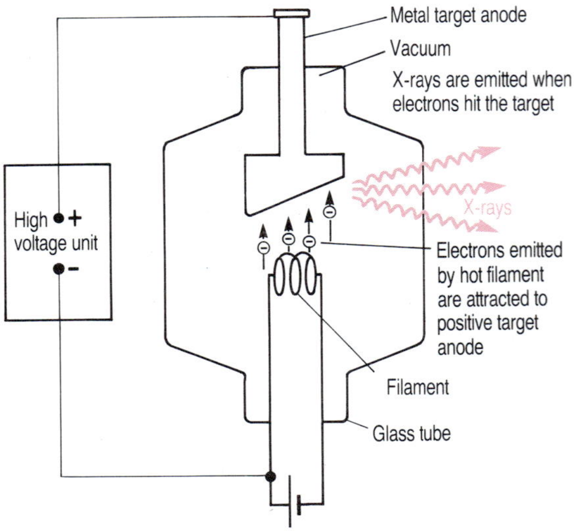

Figure 9.4 How an X-ray tube works

The X-ray tube

In an X-ray tube, a beam of electrons travelling very fast (near the speed of light) strike a metal target. Figure 9.4 shows what happens. The impact stops the electrons and they emit X-radiation. The kinetic energy of the fast-moving electrons is converted to X-ray energy.

How a radiograph is made

X-rays pass through body tissue much more easily than through bone. When X-rays are directed at a limb, an image is formed on a photographic film placed behind it.

After taking an X-ray picture the film is developed in a photographic laboratory. The developed film (or negative) shows dark and light areas. The light areas appear where no X-rays reached the film, forming an image as shown in Figure 9.5.

The beam of X-rays from an X-ray tube contains a spread of wavelengths. Longer-wavelength X-rays (called 'soft' X-rays) are more easily absorbed by tissue than short-wavelength ('hard') X-rays. Human cells are damaged when they absorb X-radiation, so the beam is passed through a metal plate before it reaches the patient. This plate removes soft X-rays to help prevent tissue damage.

The image is formed by exposing the film to X-radiation for a fixed length of time. If this time is too short, the film will be underexposed and the image will not show up very well. If the time is too long, the extra X-radiation could harm the patient.

Certain organs without bones, such as the stomach, can be X-rayed. This is done by using a **contrast medium** to absorb X-rays. The patient is given a barium meal (see Figure 9.6). This enters the stomach as part of normal digestion. The barium in the stomach shows up on the X-ray or computer screen.

The radiographer and assistants stand behind a protective lead-lined wall when an X-ray is being taken. The thick layer of lead absorbs X-radiation and prevents X-rays reaching the staff. Strict safety rules are enforced to make sure that the staff do not absorb more than a certain dose of X-radiation. They wear **film badges** to monitor their exposure to X-rays (see Figure 9.7). The badges are developed at regular intervals. If the film in a badge is overexposed, the wearer has received too much X-radiation.

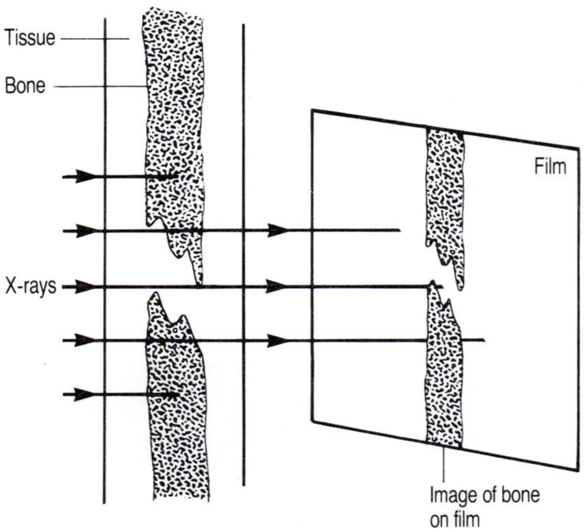

Figure 9.5 The X-ray image

Figure 9.6 Taking a barium meal for a stomach X-ray

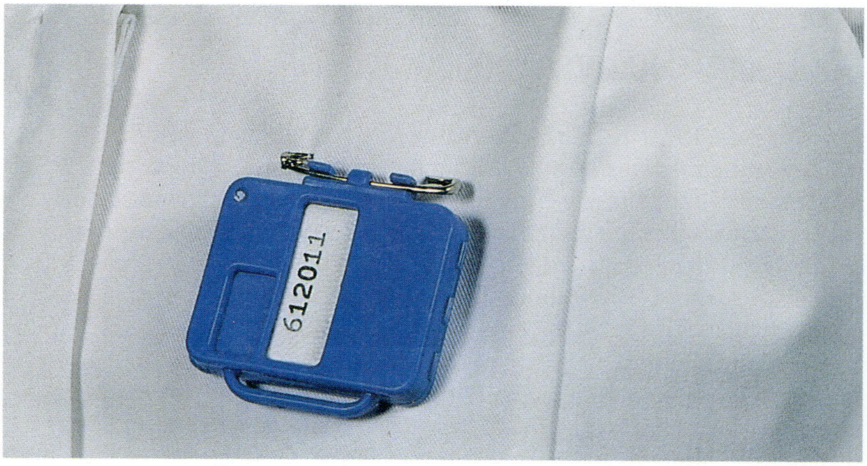

Figure 9.7 Wearing a film badge

Summary

X-rays are electromagnetic waves produced when fast-moving electrons are stopped. They pass through many materials including tissue, paper, plastic and thin layers of metals. A radiograph of a limb or organ is an X-ray photograph showing an image of the limb or organ.

Questions

1 On a radiograph of a broken arm, the break in the bone can be clearly seen, even though the skin is not broken. Explain why the break is seen on the radiograph.

2 **a** Why is a barium meal given to a patient before a stomach X-ray is taken?
b Why does the X-ray have to be taken very quickly?

3 When an X-ray is taken, the radiography staff go behind a lead-lined wall.
a Why is it dangerous for them to stay near the X-ray tube?
b Why is the protective wall lined with lead?

4 X-ray machines are used in industry to detect cracks inside metal beams. Figure 9.8 shows X-rays being used to inspect a crack in a girder.
a Why would an image of the crack show up on the developed film?
b Why is it important to detect cracks in girders used for constructing buildings?

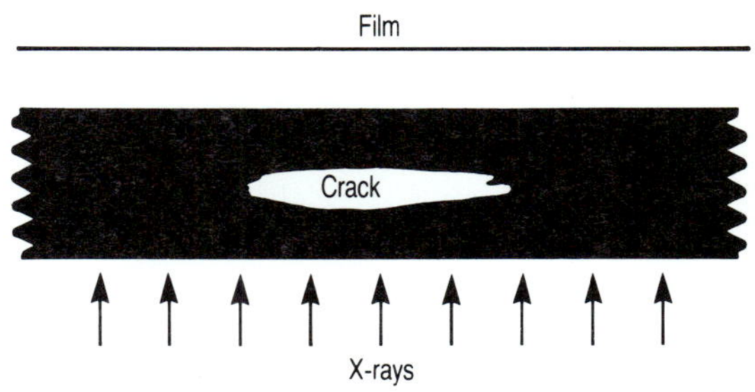

Figure 9.8

5 Airport security personnel use X-ray machines linked to television monitors to inspect bags and cases.
a Why would a weapon hidden in a bag be detected using this system?
b Why is it important to monitor passenger luggage in this way?
c Why are the X-ray machines linked to television monitors rather than using film?

Summary of equations and units

1 Prefixes

Micro- (μ) means $\times 10^{-6}$ eg 1 μA = 1 microampere = 10^{-6} A
Milli- (m) means $\times 10^{-3}$ eg 1 mA = milliampere = 10^{-3} A
Kilo- (k) means $\times 10^{3}$ eg 1 kV = 1 kilovolt = 1000 V
Meg- or Mega- (M) means $\times 10^{6}$ eg 1 MΩ = 1 megaohm = 10^{6} Ω

2 Equations

Charge, Q = current, I × time, t

Potential difference (or voltage), $V = \dfrac{\text{electrical energy delivered}}{\text{charge}}$

Electric power, P = current, I × voltage, V

Resistance, $R = \dfrac{\text{voltage, } V}{\text{current, } I}$

Heat produced by a resistor = I^2Rt where I = current, R = resistance, t = time

In series: $R = R_1 + R_2$
In parallel: $\dfrac{1}{R} = \dfrac{1}{R_1} + \dfrac{1}{R_2}$
where R is the combined resistance of two resistances R_1 and R_2

$\dfrac{\text{Secondary voltage}}{\text{Primary voltage}} = \dfrac{\text{number of secondary turns}}{\text{number of primary turns}}$ for a transformer

3 Units

The **ampere** (A), the unit of current, is the fundamental unit of electrical measurement. It is defined in terms of the force between two current-carrying conductors (see page 58). All other electrical units are derived from the ampere, as shown below.

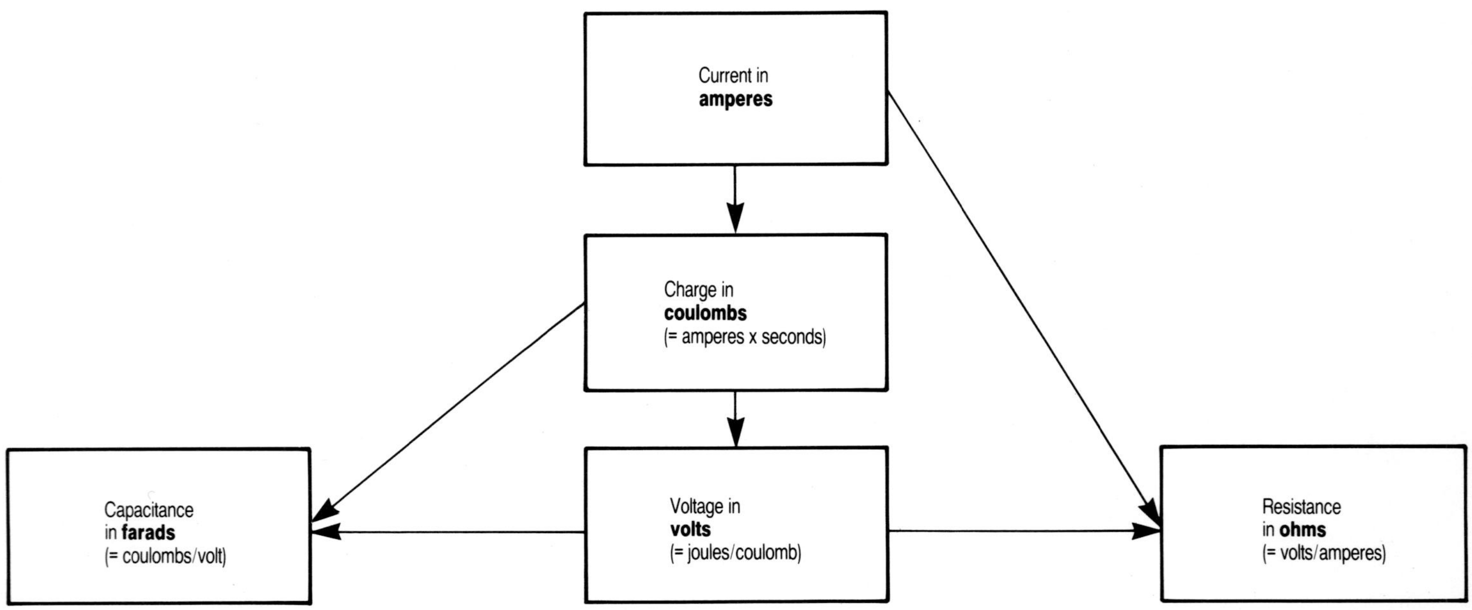

Key for Figure 4.2 (page 24)

a Cell
b Battery
c Light bulb
d Resistor
e Variable resistor
f Switch
g Ammeter
h Voltmeter
i Diode
j Light-emitting diode
k Relay (normally open)
l Light-dependent resistor
m Thermistor
n Transistor
o Capacitor
p Electrolytic capacitor
q Fuse
r Heater
s Wires not connected
t Wires connected

Index